Grace Notes

Grace Notes

RIKKI MCNEIL

Grace Notes

Copyright © 2020 by Rikki McNeil. All rights reserved.

No part of this publication may be reproduced, stored in a retrieval system or transmitted in any way by any means, electronic, mechanical, photocopy, recording or otherwise without the prior permission of the author except as provided by USA copyright law.

The opinions expressed by the author are not necessarily those of URLink Print and Media.

1603 Capitol Ave., Suite 310 Cheyenne, Wyoming USA 82001
1-888-980-6523 | admin@urlinkpublishing.com

URLink Print and Media is committed to excellence in the publishing industry.

Book design copyright © 2020 by URLink Print and Media. All rights reserved.

Published in the United States of America

ISBN 978-1-64753-297-0 (Paperback)
ISBN 978-1-64753-298-7 (Digital)

20.03.20

Dedication

This book is dedicated to my mother,
Mrs. Frankie T. McNeil

Acknowledgments

First and foremost, I would like to acknowledge God, who is the head of my life. Thank you for holding me when I thought I was all alone. Thank you for being my rock and shield in the storm. Thank you for sustaining me through every aspect of my life and for never turning your back on me.

I would like to thank Mr. Reuben Mosley. Thank you for working day and night and believing in me. Thank you for wanting the world to hear my story. I will always love you.

Thank you, Mr. Herbert Barree. You are one in a million. There has never been a time I did not come to you that you were not there, wanting nothing in return.

Thank you, Mrs. Marie Barree (godmother), for just being there for me.

And last but not least, thank you, Mrs. Deborah Reed, for being the writer. You listened to me, read my letters, and put it to paper so the world could see Rikki McNeil. May God always bless you and your family.

Contents

A Message from Deborah' Reed..11
Prologues...13

Part 1: Secrets... 17
    Secrets 1: A Love Story...18
    Secrets 2: Keeping Secrets..20

Part 2: True Confessions.. 23
    Confessions 1: My High School Sweetheart.................23
    Confession 2: A Secret Romance....................................24
    Confessions 3: The Rape...27
    Confessions 4: Common Law Lies................................31
    Confessions 5: Nightmare..34
    Confessions 6: Through the storm..................................36

Part 3: Sweet Hours of Prayer.. 40
    Sweet Hour 1: Prayer of Praise..41
    Sweet Hour 2: Prayers of Thanksgiving.......................44
    Sweet Hour 3: Prayers for the Village............................48
    Sweet Hour 4: Prayers for Protection against Evil........52
    Sweet Hour 5: Prayer for Deliverance............................55
    Sweet Hour 6: Prayers for Justice....................................60

Part 4: Trials and Tribulations.. 63
    The Shock of Trials and Tribulations............................65
    The Questions..70
    The Guilt..73

Part 5: Darkness before Dawn... 82
    Nightmare..83

Part 6:	Reap for Joy	91
	The Beginning	93
	Sowing Seeds	100
	Watering and Nourishing	103
Part 7:	Discernment and Wisdom	106
	Discernment and Wisdom for the Journey	108
Part 8:	The Mission	115
Part 9:	Bound for the Promised Land	116

A Message from Deborah Reed

Writing Rikki McNeil's story has been one of the most amazing journeys I have ever had the pleasure to undertake. Never in my wildest dreams did I ever think I would write about someone's life. Meeting Reuben Mosley for the very first time was interesting because his excitement is contagious. He was convinced that Rikki was on the verge of an exciting recording career and that God was orchestrating the entire deal. He told me to pray about writing this story and then let him know, at a later date, if I would accept the challenge. I laughed but agreed to pray and consider his request. He told me he would be back in touch with me in about two weeks.

Good to his word, Reuben called to see what I had decided. Again, I protested, telling him that I came from a traditional, classical music background at church. I was not familiar with gospel music other than old hymns. We had nothing in common except we were both Christians and we were both mothers of sons. He assured me that my background made no difference. I told him I would want to meet Rikki before committing to write anything. The arrangements were made, and Rikki came to my home one evening after work.

In no time, we were talking as though we had known each other forever. Again, I told her my concerns about never writing something this important or having ever been published except for newspaper articles. As she left my home, she said we should both pray about whether or not we were the right fit. I did pray and asked God to give me a good excuse to back out.

I called Rikki and asked her if we could meet again. We made plans again for an evening after work, and I promised to have supper waiting for her. After we ate, we settled down, and I began to listen to Rikki's story. Before she left, I knew her story needed to be told. She told me she was comfortable talking to me about her life. We met many times after that, and I always looked forward to seeing and visiting with Rikki. I was humbled as she relayed her suffering to me. I wanted to protect her, but her faith strengthened her to push on toward the goal.

Rikki's first day at the recording studio, to record her CD Just Gospel, I sat down at the computer and began writing. I called Rikki in Oklahoma. It was about seven in the evening, and she answered her cell phone. She was thrilled about her first day in the studio. I was delighted that I had started writing. We must have sounded like two schoolgirls talking for hours on the phone, oblivious to the world around us. After hanging up, I felt that God had brought two completely different people together to accomplish a mighty important task.

The task is finished for me, but for Rikki, it is just the beginning. It has been a blessing to write Rikki's story because I witnessed the power of redeeming love. I am convinced that God really did "orchestrate the entire deal." Rikki is a lovely woman filled with love for all of God's people. She trusts God with all her heart, and she is determined to live and shout for joy!

On a personal note, Rikki and Reuben, thank you for trusting me to write this incredible story. It has been my privilege to meet and work with both of you. Thanks also to Pam Pryor for suggesting me to Reuben and for listening to me as I discovered a way to tell Rikki's story. Most importantly, I thank God for the inspiration to write. I am still in awe of His mighty power to use a "nobody" to tell a story like Rikki's. Finally, Rikki McNeil, I want you to know that I will follow your story and listen to your songs all the days ahead.

Prologues

My son was murdered. I had a life before he was murdered, but how does life go on after your son is murdered? I did not participate in my life for many years after my son's murder. I continued to work, saw a psychologist, took antidepressants, went to church, sang in the choir, and attended various family celebrations, funerals, and other functions that required my presence. During this time, I did not see the sun come up or the day change into night. I did not see the leaves change colors and fall from the trees, nor did I see the daffodils poke through the spring soil. I did not feel summer's basking heat or winter's frigid cold because the seasons never changed in all that time. My ears did not hear mournful coos from the doves each morning nor choirs of angels singing carols at Christmas. My taste buds ceased to register sweet and tart flavors. I did not smell cinnamon rolls baking or notice the velvet smoothness on my tongue as a Hershey's Kiss dissolved. My fingers could peck on a keyboard, but they could not feel the beats of my own pulse. These actions that prove life is in progress ceased for me except for one essential thing: my heart continued pumping blood to all the parts of my body, though I willed it to stop. So that's how life goes on after your son is murdered. As a matter of fact, that's how life went on for over fifteen years.

Now stay tuned because I don't want to lose you in the depths of my despair. There is purpose in my story. I want to praise and sing to the glory of God all the days of my life so that you might know that all things are possible through Christ, our Lord and Savior. Yes, I am alive! I am alive, not because I overcame my grief after fifteen years, but because Christ commanded me to live. In May 2010, I was at my desk working and I slipped in a CD by a well-known pastor and biblical scholar. I put it on, filling the air with "white-noise" to help pass the time while I worked. I surely was not paying attention, nor could I tell you what it was even about. In a very odd moment, I was stunned to hear the word live. That word, live, was slowly, distinctly, and forcefully spoken in a prayer by the pastor.

The entire remainder of the day was interrupted by live. I continued to hear live. I thought about it; I tried to stop thinking about it. I was captivated and obsessed with that one word. I wondered if I had finally lost touch with reality. I could not focus on my work, frustrated by live sounding off in my head. I hollered at God, "What are you doing to me?" Even though I yelled at God and blamed him for this intrusion, suddenly the tension in my shoulders began to ebb. Maybe acknowledging God, even in my anger, was the pivotal point in restoring my life. God had placed this word in my ears, and I heard it in my heart. God commanded me to live!

After wrestling with God that day, I begrudgingly began to obey. It is strangely comforting to be in the same place for so many years. You don't have to go through change, which is a terrifying task, you don't have to anticipate, and you don't have to think too hard. I know this seems callous, but sometimes being dead while you are still alive is easier. Going through the motions means you really do not have to participate. You don't have to go through hurts and disappointments; you have no expectation, no hopes, and no dreams. That's why obeying God was tough because he required so much of me. Let me tell you right now, living is hard work! But at the end of the day, our hard work provides us with the gift of peaceful sleep. To labor in God's love is to rest in His peace.

The Bible tells us in Romans 15:4:

> "For whatever things were written for our learning, that we through the patience and comfort of the Scriptures might have hope."

By sharing my journey from the past through the valleys of darkness to life alive in Christ, I hope to encourage you to seek God, who restores all hope. The best way for me to take you on this journey is by sharing letters I have written to God. I want you to experience a little of the roller coaster I have ridden more years than

I like to acknowledge. Hopefully the only queasiness you get will just be the Holy Spirit raring to jump into your life! So this is my story and this is my song of how God commanded me to live. I hope you stay tuned.

PART 1

Secrets

For years I have written letters to God about my secrets, hoping that if I told him my secrets, he would realize how sorry I was for all the wrong things I had ever done. Writing to God was my way to divulge all the secrets that I lived. I was petrified someone would discover my secrets and expose me to the world. I have recently decided to keep my letters because they represent my own self-discovery with God as my designated explorer.

I thank God for opening the cavern of secrets in my life. I see some of these secrets as stalactites, dripping slowly downward until very little is seen yet sharp enough to stab me like a dagger through the heart. Some secrets are like stalagmites, piling one on top of the other based on lie after lie. These secrets grow and grow upward, on and on throughout your life, until there is no end, no resolution, just perpetuation of added lies. These secrets in my life stabbed me in the front during daily routines and in the back when I least expected it. No wonder I felt like I was stuck. If I tried to move forward, I was pierced through my heart. If I tried to move backward and clean up the debris, I was knifed in the back. So I prayed to God, my explorer, that he would walk with me through the hidden secrets in my life.

The reason I mention secrets is because much of my life has been lived in the midst of secrets. Some of my secrets were kept by me because I did not want anyone else to know what was going on in my life. Some secrets were kept from me. Surely those who kept secrets from me were trying to protect me, not hurt me. Even so, it was the many secrets kept from me that caused me to think something was really wrong with me. The secrecy started before my birth. My parents met under strange circumstances, though I did not learn some of these secrets until I was an adult. I always suspected that my family was different because of things I would hear at church or the way people acted toward me and my mother. I was fearful these secrets would somehow condemn me for all of eternity. Yet I was more worried about what other people would think if the secrets were exposed to them instead of God's light.

"You have set our iniquities before you, our secret sins in the light of your countenance."

Psalm 90:8

Secrets 1
A Love Story

My parents met while they were married to other people. Dad was the pastor of a church in the heart of South Dallas and married with five children. His first wife would take off and be gone for months at a time, leaving my dad to care for the children at least that was what was told to me. During one of these absences, my dad hired a new secretary for the church. That was my mother, who, at the time, was married to an abusive man. She had no children and was attending college when she started working at the church. According to bits and pieces of this secret, my father counseled with my mother about her abusive relationship. In the compassion of counseling moments, passion was kindled, and mother got pregnant with me. My mother divorced her abusive husband, but my dad could not divorce because his wife was nowhere to be found, thus the first secrets took hold. Two weeks before my birth, somehow Dad got his divorce, and my parents were married.

I'm pretty sure I was the first hated child in our church, being the offspring of the scarlet-lettered adulteress. Beyond the disdain of the church was the hatred and anger of my dad's five other children.

They disrespected my mother and resented me. I was told the older children hated my mother so much that they buried me up to my neck in the dirt. They held my mother's arms behind her while she screamed to let me go. Mother never said anything about this treacherous event, hoping that her silence would somehow appease the older children, since they could not be punished if my dad did not know about this torture. Maybe she was just scared for our safety, or perhaps they blackmailed her into not telling. Mother went on to give birth to my younger siblings, a sister and brother. I know our parents tried to make sure we kids did not know anything about their secrets, but people talk, especially in church. I never told my parents I knew the history behind their marriage. I just perpetuated their secrets.

My father took his role as pastor ever so seriously. His sermons started in a whisper so the congregation had to lean in to hear him closely, and then he would rev up louder and stronger, pitching the gospel as hard as the fastest curveball ever thrown. Listening to my father preach, I would hear him speak on the goodness of God, about forgiveness, and that God is always with us. Singing hymns at church made me feel warm and fuzzy, and I recognized I needed God. My father inspired my connection with God at an early age. He made sure that all us kids knew we were loved. He certainly made me feel special. When I was about six years old, he started traveling to revivals, and I was allowed to go with him. I was so proud to be his little girl because he was treated as a celebrity. People came from all over to hear my father preach. I knew him to be God's right-hand man.

Upon returning home from these revivals, I would think how strange it was that my mother would ask me, "Who combed your hair while you were gone?" I now realize she was just trying to find out if any other women were around my father. I'm sure her insecurities came as baggage from her first marriage. The feelings of inadequacy, coupled with all the ridicule and gossip she endured for years, led to the next secret. She started drinking, though none of us realized it. Her life must have been incredibly difficult suffering such abuse. Even her own sister, my aunt, maliciously took me to my mother's ex-husband and handed me over to him, accusing him of being my real father. Discovering the source of my mother's new pain, Father told my aunt she was no longer welcome in our home. He tenderly loved mother, even when her drinking became a problem. When she drank, she was a different person; combative and testy was not her nature. She would go to church after drinking only to be corralled, brought home by either my father or a deacon, and put to bed. This, of course, led to more tongue wagging at the church, which I was acutely aware of but did not understand. Maybe the years of abuse from my father's church and his family capsulated as secrets broke my mother's already guilt-ridden spirit.

Secrets 2
Keeping Secrets

The secrets of my birth and early family life were designed to shelter me from hurt. At least, that is what I hoped, rather than from maliciousness. Sometimes the not knowing creates scenarios that differ from reality. Though these secrets intricately wound through my childhood, I am grateful for a loving, safe home. Besides my parents and siblings, I had two grandmothers who nurtured and lovingly cared for me. Mama Jackie was my mother's mother. She was soft-spoken and soft to the touch. Her hugs melted me like sweet butter. Mama Jackie survived an abusive marriage, though she never talked about it with me. She refused to waste time on a sorrowful past. Mama Jackie was the daughter of a slave girl and her white master. She lived in East Texas. Spending time on the ranch with Mama Jackie were my fondest memories. I remember the aromas coming from her kitchen to my room.

My father could stir up soul food in the kitchen as well as from the pulpit. I remember Christmas with all the family, including aunts, uncles, and tons of cousins. We feasted and opened gifts. I remember my older sister had played with my talking doll all night until she wore the batteries down. How funny the family thought it was when I opened up my gift from Santa and my baby doll could not talk. My mother would play the piano, and the rest of us would sing. I loved our singing at home with my mother. Seeing her happy made me happy. No wonder I was drawn to music at such a young age. Her mother also played the piano. I didn't even know what rapture meant, but surely music was the way to heavenly bliss. All of my family could sing, so I was not especially singled out as the next music virtuoso; however, I can remember singing at church, at home, in the car, walking, and, of course, in the tub. I must thank you, Lord, for putting music in my heart and soul. I haven't always known, but I am sure music in song is my direct link to you, God.

My other grandmother was my godmother. I don't know how she became my grandmother, but we all accepted her in this position. Mama Jackie, my real grandmother, whom I adored, and my god-grandmother, fondly named Gee-Gee, were huge influences in my life. Gee-Gee loved music too. She loved to dance. We would get up on Sunday morning, turn on the radio to gospel music, and just have a great time holy dancing, Gee-Gee was the ray of sunshine for our family and the pillar of strength for many years. Her faith could mend many a broken spirit. She pushed forward, grateful for each new morning of life. She taught me endurance and to make the best out of a bad situation. Though Gee-Gee participated in far too many secrets, she was the stabilizing backbone in our family. She always had time for a prayer. Amen.

My sister and little brother were very important to me growing up. We fought like all siblings. We played, shared, and cared for one another. I always thought I was closest to my father. He was my hero and protector. My sister seemed closest to my god-grandmother. I think she doted on her more than me. Of course, my brother was my mother's favorite. In her eyes, he could do no wrong. The weird thing is that in my mind I always thought my brother and sister were privy to the secrets of our family, even though I was the oldest. I know this is like a conspiracy theory, but really, God, I grew up thinking I was an outcast. Here was this family circle, and sometimes I felt on the outside, aware that secrets did exist. That's how I learned not to talk about things in my life that weren't smooth.

Well, God, this is just a little synopsis about my childhood. I know you know everything and more, but maybe examining my beginnings will help the discovery of my purpose in your great plan. I was aware of you in my early conscience, and I am grateful that my father and mother raised me in a Christian home. They certainly planted the seed, small as a mustard seed, but still love and faith flourished in our home.

PART 2
True Confessions

~~~~~~~~~~~~~~~~~~~~~~~~~~~~~~~~~~~~

"Confession is good for the soul," so says an ancient Scottish proverb. Some confessions are tantalizing as proven by the magazine True Confessions, launched in 1992, or the novel True Confessions by John Dunne, or, even later, the movie by the same name, starring Robert DeNiro. I'm not sure if my confessions are tantalizing. Mine are just confessions of a misguided, "looking for love in all the wrong places" heart. Naturally, my true confessions are top secret and have been hidden away and forgotten like discarded junk in the basement of my heart, covered with years of dankness, in the hope of never dredging up tarnished memories.

It is written, "If we confess our sins, He is faithful and just to forgive us our sins and to cleanse us from all unrighteousness" (1 John 1:9). I was not sure about exposing these secrets because the fear of guilt and pain could push them back into the dark portals of denial. I trusted in you, the Lord, the light of the world, to shed light on my confessions in order to throw out the unnecessary clutter and make room for the new renovations you, O God, desired for me.

Confessions 1
My High School Sweetheart

We were seventeen years old and attended the same high school. He was a star basketball player, popular and very handsome. He was doted on by his family because he was the youngest. I would go to his games and feel special being his girlfriend. He would come to my home and have dinner with my family. They liked Alvin and approved of my first love. We went to movies, church, and school dances together. We talked for hours on the phone. I couldn't bear to get off the phone at night when my grandmother would tell me, "Say good night; you've got school in the morning. "The only thing that kept me from collapsing in a puddle of tears was that the next morning I would see Alvin coming over to walk me to school. Life was wonderful and dramatic as the fairy tale. I was convinced he was my Prince Charming. We would live forever in the Magic Kingdom.

Our growing love aroused newly developed hormones. The red-hot passion of ours had to mean true love, and that meant sex. I truly thought having sex was making love with Alvin. The lovemaking assured us of "happily ever after." Instead, I got pregnant the first time we made love. I was now just another statistic.

Confession 2
A Secret Romance

During my romance with Prince Charming, before I knew about the pregnancy, my interest in "happily ever after" fizzled. For some reason, and I am not sure why, I just no longer had the same feelings for Alvin. He did nothing wrong; he was the same person I fell in love with. He really tried to make our marriage work. But I had already fallen in love with another young man. I was flattered by the flirtations of an older boy from another high school. It was like tasting the forbidden fruit. I knew Alvin and I were meant to be exclusive lovers, but the thought of an older guy was tempting. Sammy was irresistible, electrifying, and so much fun. We met secretly at first, and then I fell madly in love with him. He was my true love, not Prince Charming. I had made a dreadful mistake. After all, how could I stay away from the knight in shining armor when my every breath desired to inhale him? My newly found, lustful love lasted only a short while after I discovered I was pregnant with Alvin's baby. My "two-timing" days ended when my father decreed a wedding would take place quickly before the baby was born. According to my father, a child could not be born without the sanctity of marriage. My mother knew I was in love with Sammy, but she fully supported my father's decision. She flew into elaborate preparations for a grand wedding.

This drama could have won an Oscar. There was crying and pleading with my dad, his absolute authority of doing things properly, and my mother frantically consoling me while she tied flowers to the pews at church. Oh my Lord, talk about a frenzy. It sure is funny how a person's life can suddenly become so unmanageable.

What is it about weddings that bring out the best and the worst in people? My entire family was involved in the wedding preparations. My grandmother made my wedding dress, and my sister, along with a good friend, shopped for the bridesmaids' dresses. Momma and Gee-Gee decorated and set up the reception hall. I was not involved with any of the plans, nor did I want to be.

I spent most of the time crying in my room. I was being forced to marry a boy I did not love. Also, I was very much aware that I was a disappointment to my family, especially my father. I can't even imagine how disappointed you, O God, must have been with me.

The day of the wedding came. The church was beautiful and filled with guests all dressed up in their Sunday's best. I arrived late to church. Holding back my own tears, I heard my sister and cousin crying as they stood beside me at the altar. I could hear my grandmother from her pew on the front row crying and uttering under her breath that my father was going to regret his decision to make me marry. I cannot remember the vows that were spoken. I was shattered. After all, my "happily ever after" was not going to happen. Instead, I was a brokenhearted little girl, lost and afraid, stepping out on a journey to places completely uncharted.

After the wedding, I went home with my parents, unaccompanied by my new husband. I had no idea where he went, but for sure my father found him. He moved into my parents' home the next day. We continued to live with my parents for about three months. During this time, I tried to live up to my dad's expectations for being his good little girl, but I sank deeper into the murky waters of unhappiness.

My father told me, "You will learn to love him. He is now your husband." I tried, but I could not do as he instructed. I was torn between my own anguish, unhappiness, and the disappointment of my father. Eventually Daddy did recognize the marriage was doomed, but he continued to show his disfavor. He seldom would speak with me, and when he did, it would be in anger or condemnation, often calling me "Jezebel." Our home was filled with tension and icy glares.

After playing house for those three months, my beloved husband moved out, declaring he was not the father of my unborn baby. Our son was born in March 1972 at St. Paul's Hospital in Dallas. This was the scariest day of my life. I felt so alone, thinking my mother was the only one who cared enough to come to the hospital. She did not tell me until later that my father was there for the delivery but would not come into my room to see me. She explained he was hurt because he had high hopes for me, and I had disappointed him by getting pregnant out of wedlock. Mommy often smoothed things over between my dad and me.

In the hours following my son's birth, a new determination to be both a good mother and a source of pride for my father grew in me. Filled with enthusiasm and excitement for this new challenge, I headed back to school, got a job, and divorced my son's father. I was going to do the best I could with my life.

Even with my new resolve, I continued to see my secret love, and he helped me get on my feet to start down the new road I wanted to travel. My first priority was to get a divorce from Alvin as quickly as possible. Sammy gave me money to go along with my first paycheck so I could file for the divorce. While I was at work or school, Sammy and his family would keep my son. Our late nights together were blissful. Things were looking up!

Child support was minimal and did not continue for long. I did not want my son to be around a father who had not accepted responsibility for his son and who continued to deny paternity. I often cried, staring at my baby son because the resemblance to his father was undeniable. I did not want him in my son's life. He was not deserving of my precious son. Besides, I was afraid he would hurt Jeremy in a fit of anger toward me. Although it is typical for mothers to be protective of their children, I became overly diligent with Jeremy's safety and welfare. Was I consciously projecting the violence to come in his life, holding this tiny babe in my arms?

My plans for building a new life were in motion for about a year when I decided to end my relationship with Sammy. Though we had been through much together, and I did love him; I think we outgrew each other. I am grateful for his love and care during this transition of moving into adulthood. I still think of him as my first real love, my knight in shining armor, who rescued me from the dragons of my youth.

Confessions 3
The Rape

I'm not quite sure how to begin this confession, but surely, God, you know my heart. I have tried time and time again to find the right man. Every woman should learn to wait on you to pick out the right man. It seems like I cannot pick out a good man to save my life, and believe me, this next man nearly cost me my life!

I was working at a bank in downtown Dallas and going to school to become a teacher like my mother. By the way, I didn't like school. I took only the minimum hours to meet the department's requirements. My life was very predictable with classes, work, tending to my son, and, of course, church and choir. I was happy in my busy world. I was striving for my father's approval and trying to be a good provider for my son.

Then it happened. I met Devon, a student at a local college with a great singing voice. He appeared handsome, suave, and sophisticated. We met at church during a choir program. I quickly determined he had to be Mr. Right. What's not to be right? Good education, church, choir-what more could anyone want? It didn't take long to discover how wrong and dangerous this decision was.

Here was the reality: he was an abuser. His smooth talking class act did not last long when the beating began. At first it was just a shove. Then he grabbed at my hair to get my attention. Shockingly, he beat me with chains and club sticks. He would scream and yell at me, curse, and belittle me. After harshly reprimanding my son with a spanking, I could no longer allow my son to be around him. I don't know why I did not stop dating him right then, because things quickly escalated.

I found out he had another girlfriend at the same time he dated me. She came to church one day and announced she was pregnant with his baby and they were going to be married. I didn't really feel betrayed because we weren't married, and the abuse was worsening. Though I did not have proof, I suspected he was using illegal drugs. He acted like a wild man at times, raging in anger and jealousy. After two years, I ended the relationship, but Devon was not finished with me.

Here I was, God, gaining confidence and rebuilding my self-esteem after this fiasco of a relationship. That's when the stalking began. He wouldn't leave me alone, showing up at school or while I was at work. He called all hours of the day and night, and this scared me. I was sharing an apartment with my cousin. We were both asleep one night when he broke in. He beat me, held me down, and raped me. I did not report the rape to anyone. Who would believe me? After all, we had dated. My track record was not great, and no one knew how mean he really was or about the beatings.

I became physically ill; I only wanted to sleep and cry. My family did not know what was happening because I was too ashamed to tell them. Nobody was going to find out my dirty little secret. I grew weaker and weaker; seldom did I get out of bed because my legs felt like jelly. My head hurt, and there was lots of bleeding. I couldn't eat without vomiting; in fact, I began to lose weight. Once, I asked for help from my cousin. She responded by throwing me a hot water bottle that landed on the floor. She may have thought I was just moping around, or she wouldn't have been so unkind. Falling from my bed to retrieve the hot water bottle, I thought about dying.

Surely death would quiet the ache in my heart and the agony of my deteriorating body.

After being in bed for about two weeks, an angel appeared. Cyndie Lynn-an old friend I had not seen in years-called, and I actually answered the phone. She said, "Rikki, God put you in my heart today. I didn't know how to get in touch with you, but I called Vanelle-a family friend—and she gave me your number. How are you? Are you all right?"

I whispered back, "No, girlfriend. I'm not so good." O God, thank you for watching out for me.

Cyndie Lynn calmly said, "How do I get to your apartment? I'm on my way."

Comforted, I managed to give her directions, and within minutes, she appeared at my bedside. Wrapping a blanket around me, she gathered me up in her arms and somehow carried me to her car. This angel of mercy drove me straight to the hospital. She stayed beside me for what seemed like an eternity that day.

The news was not good. The tests revealed I was pregnant from the rape, and because of the excessive bleeding, the baby was in danger. If that wasn't shock enough, my friend and I learned the pregnancy was complicated by another problem. I was diagnosed with sickle-cell disease.

I was dazed to hear the doctor's discourse about a disease of the red blood cells causing abnormal hemoglobin and anemia. He said that sickle cells multiply quickly, cutting off the blood supply, causing terrible pain, organ damage, stroke, infections, and even blindness. With the anemic crisis, my pregnancy was not an option. The doctor grimly looked at my friend, Cyndie Lynn. He suggested she call my family because the next few hours were critical; I could die! O God, was this really happening?

Things whirled around me after the news. I was rushed into a sterile room for some kind of procedure that ended the pregnancy. I was put in ICU, hooked up to monitors, and had a blood transfusion. It seemed like I was floating in some kind of fog. I wondered if this was a dream or maybe I was delusional, especially after waking up to see my father praying at my bedside with my mother next to him. I thought for sure I was having an out-of-body experience. My angel friend had indeed called my family, and they came.

In those days, I don't think many people knew about sickle-cell disease, including my family. My mother and father did not ask many questions; instead, my father picked me up and took me home with them. He arranged for prayer vigils. Family and church members offered their prayers around the clock, asking prayers for my healing. Once during a prayer session, I overheard my mother whispering to my father, "Why are you praying for her? She is going to die. Just let her die."

O God, did Mommy know what happened to me? Did she know about the rape? Had she told my father? In my delusional and weakened state, I thought she wanted me to die as punishment for the rape, the pregnancy, and aborting the fetus. Probably my death would be better for everyone. I never told. I never told my father about the rape or the pregnancy. I was so ashamed. Once again, I let my father down, and I was sure I had let you down, God. I'm sure you were tired of seeing the sins of my life. How could you ever use me?

One day weeks later, regaining my strength little by little, I got dressed and rode to the church with my father. I told him I was feeling better. With my health improving, remorse began to invade my thoughts. Once inside his office, I sat down and began to cry, unburdening-only certain parts-of my soul to him. I told him how sorry I was for all the pain I had caused him with my poor choices and actions. We talked about sin and the consequences. I promised him—and you,

God—that I was going to change my life and become a better person. I wanted my father to be proud of me. I wanted you, Lord, to be the master of my heart. I don't have to tell you how long my promise lasted.

Confessions 4
Common Law Lies

You probably think this next true confession came straight out of the tabloids, and it is one of the oddest. By this time, several years had passed since my last fiasco of a relationship. My health had returned, and things seemed better with my family. I felt secure thinking that all the prayers of my father, mother, and the church had surely been answered. I was a special child saved by the power of prayer and loved by my family and friends. My son was also thriving, and life was beautiful. What else could anyone ask for?

Here I was again, looking for love in all the wrong places. I started dating, telling myself to take it easy. At first, William and I had so much fun together. We did everything together, and before I knew it, I thought, Okay, this is it, the real deal.

My father was not impressed with this guy, and he voiced his displeasure soon after we started seeing each other. Of course, I figured my father wouldn't like any guy I ever brought home. No man could live up to his expectations for a proper mate for his precious daughter. I argued with my father, "Come on, Dad. After all, he goes to church. I get along great with his family. He's the best."

Disregarding my father's concern, I proceeded to fall in love with William. We really had a good relationship for about four years when the downward plunge started. I got pregnant, and we were not married. Being well known in our community and church, because of the recognition from my gospel singing, I lied. I told everyone we were married. William went along with this deceit because he had no intention of marrying me, but the lie served its purpose well, as I later discovered.

Spiraling downhill, the relationship took a number of jolting knocks that slammed against my heart. First came the night I cried for joy at the birth of my baby daughter, only to be thrown into uncontrolled sobbing as the nurse tore her from my arms. She was dead. My baby girl died at birth. Panicking because somehow my lie had taken the breath away from this little angel, I was heavily sedated. Sinking into a drugged refuge of sleep for days, I was not aware my mother took my baby girl and had her properly buried in a cemetery with a small grave marker. To this day, Lord, I do not know where my baby girl is buried. In later years, I was told my mother and my son would often go and clean off my baby's grave and put out flowers. They kept all of this from me. Another secret. Surely they were trying to protect me from the pain. My mother's compassion and love during this time comforted me.

The spiraling down into deep sadness was affected by two other events that occurred during this same time span. The first was the death of my father, my rock, my hero, my friend. I think my father had a premonition because I remember he announced at church, "I'm not going to be with you for much longer." He died within the month following that statement.

Grief swept over me like the angel of death. I had let this amazing man down time and time again. He loved my son and was really the only father Jeremy ever knew. For sure my future was in jeopardy without the stability of my father's love and prayers. I never felt I got enough opportunities to assure him of my love and my desire to be what he wanted. I feared my father's death foreshadowed my own doomed pathway to the grave. Even worse, I feared losing other family members I loved. In my own despair, I could scarcely console my son's pain at the loss of his grandfather, even though he was so young. I lost my father, and Jeremy lost his grandfather. He was the only good man in both our lives. I heard it said that trouble comes in threes, and this proved to be true.

The third broke my heart all over again. Struggling after losing my baby daughter and my dad, I received a call from my stepbrother late one afternoon. Jerry was the only step-sibling my mother and I really got along with, and he had been kind enough to visit me in the hospital. His call was not good news. He needed open-heart surgery, and he was scared he would die. I offered him my prayers, stunned that he even had heart problems. After his surgery, I was on my way to visit him in the hospital, but I did not make it in time before he passed away from complications.

This confession ends with a bizarre twist as the lie grew out of control with William. As I said before, the lie about us being married served him very well. We were known in our community, and I was performing more and more at church. I was building a good reputation as a gospel singer. Our life looked perfectly packaged to everyone, including me. It's funny how you begin to believe a lie is true. That truth came crashing down the day I came home, unexpectedly, and found my dear mate with another man. I nearly lost my mind, sitting in our home waiting two hours before they realized I was there in the house. I sat on the sofa wondering what to say or do. Evidence of drugs was everywhere. My head was spinning with thoughts of humiliation and shame. I realized he was using me as a screen for his family and the community. What now? Should I murder him by strangling him, or should I leave?

William tried to convince me to stay. I knew this was only to protect his reputation. I was through living in this lie. Ironically, we had to go through a divorce because we owned property together. After hiring a lawyer and filing for divorce, I discovered he had created enough debts to open up another Wall Street bank. When it was all said and done, I walked away with nothing but the shirt on my back, and I was lucky to have it.

My son was about twelve years old then, and he didn't have much to do with William. Jeremy did not spend nights with us if William was at the house. Maybe Jeremy sensed something was wrong with William or he knew more than I could imagine.

God, this confession proved to be painful. This was a time of much anguish, sadness, loss, anger, and insecurity. Once again, promises were made to change my life for the better. I wanted to prove myself to you and my daddy, but how was I going to overcome these troubles and start life anew? How could I be worthy enough?

Confessions 5
Nightmare

Just when you've come through a major life lesson and you think, I'll never do it again, beware! Now, I'm sure, Lord, that you were frustrated with me waiting to surrender, but as fate would have it, I grew bored and lonely. My sister introduced me to my next mistake because it was time for me to move on with my life. She still tells me to this day, "I just wanted you to go out and have fun, not marry the guy."

Why do women think we have to be with someone? Why do we get so lonesome? Why do we need a replacement to get over the last guy? Is it because the love we are looking for just doesn't fix us? Repair us? Make us whole? Whatever the reason, I jumped into another catastrophe. I didn't really even like this man. He was a liar from the start, telling me he was not married. It took only three months to discover this lie, and I should have run for the hills. In my pathetic want of a man's attention, I bought in to the lie and became part of it.

He had me thinking he was being wronged by the entire world. He was another smooth talker, convincing and eloquent. The poor "victim" fought back against the world and all its woes by beating me and threatening me and my family. He hurled horrible, demeaning words at me. Instead of escaping this tyrant, I married Oscar at the courthouse right after his divorce was finalized. He was jubilant, and I was sick to my stomach. I had done the wrong thing again, for sure.

This nightmare lasted for about seven years. He had trouble holding on to jobs because of pursuing drugs, alcohol, and other women. I was working for a huge furniture company, had been promoted, and was making fairly good money. He was in and out of rehabs that cost me plenty. More than once he showed up drunk at my job, looking for money, and my supervisor had to call security. My mother bought him a truck. Deceiving all of us, the police were called, and he reported the truck stolen. He probably traded it for drugs or scammed the insurance company.

My son despised Oscar. Though I never told my son or my family about the abuse, I'm sure they were aware and alarmed. On one occasion, he put a gun to my head and pulled the trigger. I knew it was only by your grace, Lord, that I lived. The beatings continued, and he would steal from my purse or from my family. Why didn't I leave? I couldn't because of the threats to my son and other family members.

So frightened of harm coming to my family, I went to my grandmother, confessing to her my fears about Oscar. She told me we would have to pray him away, because if I left him, he would surely kill me. We both knelt down together and began to pray. I prayed harder than ever before, "God, deliver me."

Grandmother prayed, "Lord, hear my prayers----prayers that will not stop until you protect Rikki. It is my mission to pray unceasingly for her deliverance from this evil." My grandmother's faith and trust in you sustained me with newfound courage. She was a beacon of your light in the world.

The following day, I believe Oscar came to my job to kill me. He came in cursing and causing a ruckus. My supervisor wanted to call the police, but I told her, "No. It won't do any good. They'll just put him in jail, and in no time, he'll get out and come after me or my family."

I didn't want him to hurt anyone, but the threat of violence was escalating. I started walking toward the backdoor near the loading docks. Raging and cursing, Oscar followed me outside. I'm positively convinced that you, my Savior, sent an angel to protect me, for at that moment, I was provided with both deep resolve and a quieted spirit. I had no way of knowing if this was the end. Was this my day of judgment? Turning to look over my shoulder, I waited for him to attack me. I screamed out, "I can't do this anymore, Oscar!"

Stunned, he stopped and stared at me with disbelieving eyes and dared me to move. I waited for my life to play out before me, convinced he was going to kill me. Instead, he turned around and walked away, and I never saw him again.

Thank you, God, for hearing my grandmother's persistent pleas for deliverance. I promised you, as long as I lived, I would sing your praises, because you heard our prayers and you answered me with protection on that horrible day.

Finally, now I knew my Savior was always with me. I no longer needed to find someone to love me because you, O God, loved me. I wanted to always trust you with every part of my life. You know my needs and my desires, and you alone will determine my relationships. Bishop Jeffery Thomas Sr. from my church said at my Bible Study, "God will not restore what we never were intended to have." I have been delivered from evil. The nightmare has ended. To you, O God, be the glory.

Confessions 6
Through the storm

I have to confess, my life with Panama Jack was slightly one-sided. Yes, he did have another girl in another city. Yes, he was a real "macho man." He was the decisionmaker. He enjoyed having the final answer. He could sweet talk vinegar into honey and make lemonade out of lemons. He was handsome as the day is long.

We visited on the phone at first and then in person at the store when he came to town on business. We started out as good friends. He worked in another city for the same company at the corporate office. He was supportive of me in business, and I looked forward to seeing this delightful man. When he was transferred to my city, it was no surprise when we started dating. For the first time, I felt respected and honored by a man. He took me to lovely restaurants or he would cook me fabulous dinners. I was living the good life. I had no clue the direction our relationship would travel as Panama Jack would soon take the helm during the worst storm of my life.

We had been enjoying each other's company for about three months when the winds of hell blew my life apart. It was 9:30 p.m., January 31, 1995. I was at church when the call came from my grandmother.

"Come home! Something is wrong with Jabbo (my son's nickname). Come home!" she cried out in panic.

A heavy, sinking feeling pushed down to the pit of my stomach. I began to sweat and salivate; the nausea rose up and then plummeted down like huge ocean waves. At first I did not move; fear held me captive.

"Rikki, come home!" Gee-Gee screamed again and again into the phone.

The adrenaline began to pump and pour into my paralyzed body. I stepped one foot in front of the other, hesitantly at first. Quickly picking up speed, I sprinted, and then running...running... I fled from the church with family and a friend following me. I have no memory of the streets I traveled or the speed I drove. I just had to get to my grandmother's house.

Turning the corner a block from her house, I slammed on the brakes at the sight of an ambulance with its lights blazing like a strobe. Surrounding the area were police cars with more lights flashing red. Throngs of people were mulling around as if they were strolling down the midway at the state fair, slowing down to see what sideshow had come to town. Bewildered, I saw my mother coming toward me, pushing through the crowd. She was crying. She looked frantic to reach me. I couldn't hear what she was saying at first. I don't even remember what she said exactly. I was immersed in the turbid waters of despair.

My son was ripped away from me. I did not hold him in my arms when he breathed his last breath. I heard him choke on his first gulp of air, followed by bellowing cries the day he was born into this world. But on this night, my ears never got the chance to hear the final breath of his life. I never heard the deep, slow melody of air as it whooshed away from my world. I don't know if he gasped like he did at birth or if he breathed in cool, clean air one last time and then gently exhaled all life.

Some deaths are silent and calm, almost sacred, like when an elderly person in hospice meets his maker. Not so with my son's death. His life was stolen through one hideous and vile act. My baby was slain with bullets shot from behind, aimed at his head, his back, and his legs. He was executed. Jabbo was murdered, dead. He was gone forever, never to be seen or heard again. I would never hear the front door squeak open with shouts of glee, "Rich, are you here?"

There are no words to describe the violation of my soul, my mind, my body. My son's sweet breath was snuffed out, stolen from me by wicked and depraved thieves in the night. No torture in the world could compare. I cannot comprehend what you, O Lord, may have endured at the moment your Son died, taking the sins of the world and separating from you, his father, at Calvary. In the moment of my son leaving this world, I was alone, oblivious to any human touch. I was betrayed and abandoned, never wanting for life again. O God, did you feel that way too?

During the debacle of the following days, I had little recall. I felt orphaned in a world to which I did not wish to retain membership, so Panama Jack paid my dues for years. He cooked nourishing meals for me. He did the laundry and the shopping. On one occasion, I was so ill that I could not get out of bed. Panama Jack got me up, bathed and dressed me appropriately, and even drove me to my job. He saw to it that the bills were paid, usually out of his own pockets. He took me to church and tried to interest me in a myriad of activities. I think he felt it was his responsibility to jumpstart my life over again. God, I'm pretty sure you had a hand in providing the kindness, gentleness, and protective spirit of Panama Jack in those days. I confess I was not aware that goodness and grace actually existed. My world was cold, dark black, and ugly.

My family was thankful to have Panama Jack in our family, though we never married. My son never got an opportunity to meet him, but I'm sure the two would have hit it off. His commitment as a friend was powerful. He stabilized my fragile raft through the engulfing tsunami of my life. He tended to me as he would a prized garden, and—being a master gardener he stepped from the role of friend to lover.

As I said at the beginning of this confession, our relationship was one-sided, not because he had a girlfriend on the side, but because I was unable to give or receive love. Now sometimes my old human nature would stir up feelings of jealousy when he was away on business, yet I did not question Panama Jack, as his intentions were so honorable. He provided admirably for me, though I seldom acknowledged his deeds. For seven years, he kept me from falling off the bow of my boat. He was my life support, though at the time I probably would have preferred being disconnected. The thought of falling from the boat into the cold, dark abyss of an ocean was soothing and enticing

I like to think our relationship ended stamped with "Job Complete." Mr. Panama Jack had protected me from the gawkers, from the circus of ex-husbands, and the hurtful church whisperers, and he tenderly bandaged my wounds. He was honest along the way, never denying his penchant for other women, especially one in particular. He was not going to marry me, but I figured he would marry her if I released him from our contract. Panama Jack deserved a real lover to share his life, so I untied the rope to my sturdy dock and set sail on a solo voyage. Though we continued on as friends for years, and once in a while we sampled a rekindled romance, the time finally came when Mr. Panama's courageous job in the storm was completed, a job well done indeed!

God, only because you have called on me to live anew can I look back and thank you for Mr. Panama Jack. The ride was rough for him, up one swell and slammed down the next. It took a strong man with a merciful spirit to ride waves like mine. I pray your blessings on the good man and ask you to make his sailing smooth. Thank you, Lord Jesus, for Mr. Panama Jack.

PART 3
Sweet Hours of Prayer

As a child, I prayed at supper, "Lord, we thank you for this food we are about to receive. Amen."

At church, I prayed, "Our Father, who art in heaven, hallowed be thy name. Thy kingdom come, thy will be done on earth as it is in heaven. Give us this day our daily bread, and forgive us our trespasses, as we forgive those who trespass against us. And lead us not into temptation, but deliver us from evil. For thine is the kingdom and the power and the glory forever. Amen."

Delaying the inevitable bedtime, I would holler for my mamma or my father to come hear my prayer: "Now I lay me down to sleep. I pray the Lord my soul to keep. God bless Mommy, Daddy, and Gee-Gee and Mommy Jackie, Aunt Emma, and Aunt Zep, and...' You get the picture. Even now, I still find joy and peace in these same prayers.

Prayers of a lifetime weave through the struggling lows and the rapturous highs, creating a tapestry of brilliant colors and textures. Some reflect pastel shades of peace, while others paint flaming reds of hurt and anger, and still others resemble somber blues. Some are soft and silken, and others are coarsely rough, depending on life's flow over the rocky rapids or the gentle trickling toward still waters. God, I believe my prayers are an outward expression of an inward relationship with you. I pray my prayers are not a oneway dialogue, just as our relationship is not one-way. I pray that I may express my heart while you listen and respond. Hopefully my prayers include my listening and my response to you.

Likewise, the Spirit also helps in our weakness. For we do not know what we should pray for as we ought, but the Spirit himself makes intercession for us with groaning that cannot be uttered. Now he who searches the heart knows what the mind of the Spirit is, because he makes intercession for the saints according to the will of God.

Romans 8:26 & 27

Sweet Hour 1
Prayer of Praise

I do not think there is a sweeter prayer of praise than the moment a baby is born and takes his first breath of air. This is a miracle moment. Moms and you, O God, partner up nine months before to grow a new life. Some moms enjoy pregnancy, looking beautiful and healthy and delighted to buy maternity clothes. Other moms hate every moment of morning sickness, extreme weight gain, acne, and moodiness. No matter the type, when the final push is made and that baby comes bursting into this world, all moms are caught up in that special moment of praising you, our God, the Creator. "Praise God from whom all blessings flow!"

Let's face it; I was one of the moms who did not particularly enjoy my pregnancy. It wasn't because I was sick with nausea or any of the aforementioned reasons. I was simply unhappy. I was not married to a man I loved or who loved me, nor would he love our baby since he denied being the father. I was miserable because I had disappointed my father by getting pregnant before I was married and failed at a marriage I was supposed to make work. Now I admit to being a bit cranky and moody because of the pregnancy. In reality, I used it as an excuse for my unhappiness to project my misery.

I had a close friend, who I often referred to as my play-sister, and a cousin who were both pregnant at the same time as I. We compared notes on every aspect of the pregnancy because we were all young and had no idea what to expect. Most of the time, they laughed and were thoroughly intrigued with the process. I, on the other hand, shrugged with boredom. I actually resented their excitement and delight in the details of every week and month. They were thankful and thrilled by every stage. I was lost in misery. My mother and grandmother tried to excite me by decorating a sweet nursery. My lack of enthusiasm grieved them both. Looking back, I regret not relishing every moment.

It was my due date and time for a doctor's appointment. My pregnant comrades and I met for lunch at Wyatt's Cafeteria before the appointment. I was starved and ate like it was my last meal. That was the one thing I did take delight in: I enjoyed eating for two. We joked at lunch that we all probably ate enough to give birth to an entire army!

After lunch, my girlfriends accompanied me to the doctor's appointment. Being in a fairly good mood for a change, I stepped on the scales and laughed. The nurse showed me to the examination room, looked at me with a scowl, and asked, "Are you in labor?" I thought what a jerk and retorted back angrily, "Do I look like I'm in labor?"

I must have looked like I was in labor because the doctor, after his exam, sent me straight to the hospital. The girls went with me. We had a good laugh because the admitting nurse, staring at three pregnant girls, said, "Okay, which one of you are in labor?"

After being admitted to the labor ward, things got a little scary. My back started to kill me. They called it "back labor." I thought my back was breaking and I hadn't even toted a child around yet. The pains started getting worse, and death was surely pending, Fortunately, my mother came to the hospital soon after I called her in tears. Trying to soothe me, she started praying and reading the Bible to me. Mother was visibly moved to tears. She said it was because her baby was in pain and her baby was having a baby. I heard that a mother forgets the pains of labor, and to some extent, I have forgotten, but I will never forget my mother's distress from my pain. My father was praying for me too, though I did not know he was there. Pain and prayers go together like a mother's kiss on a bruise. I labored all night.

It was time, March 2, 1972. The doctor came, the nurses coached, and my mother prayed at my bedside. At 6:00 a.m. the next morning, my son was born. I looked at him as the doctor proudly raised him up into the air, celebrating his maleness. A nurse took him, wiped him off a bit, and placed him in my arms naked and crying in protest. I don't recall him feeling wet, greasy, or small. I do remember smelling his sweet breath as he released the air out with each whimper. That baby's breath, I could feel it on my neck. I inhaled it like a fresh lily in spring, wanting more and more fragrance. I could hear his breath when he stopped crying. It was steady and assuring, and I could not get enough. He was breathing. You, sweet Jesus, breathed life into my son. I held a new creation, all of six pounds six ounces, ready to be embraced by the world and loved by you and me.

I praise you, Lord, for creating mankind. I praise you for creating a woman like me to carry and give birth to a precious baby boy. In my wildest dreams, I never imagined your handiwork could be so majestic in every detail, even his sweet breath. Lord, I want to sing to you a new song, praising you, declaring your glory, your splendor, and your holiness. On the day my baby, Jeremy Jerrod Johnson, was born, I was in the presence of you, God Almighty, smelling the sweetest breath of new life. We made a good team bringing that baby into this world.

Make a Joyful shout to the Lord, all you lands! Serve the Lord with gladness; Come before His presence with singing. Know that the Lord, He is God, it is He who has made us, and not we ourselves; We are His people and the Sheep of His pasture. Enter into His gates with thanksgiving, And into His courts with praise, Be thankful to Him, and bless His name. For the Lord is good; His mercy is everlasting, And His truth endures to all generations.

Psalm 100

Sweet Hour 2
Prayers of Thanksgiving

Things are chaotic and confusing after a baby is born. I was in the hospital for three days because my blood pressure was a problem. Consequently, I was not able to be with my baby, and this worried me. Was there something wrong with him? I cried when the nurse brought the babies down the hall to be fed by the mothers. Everyone got a baby except for me. I cried until my mother took me to the nursery to see my baby. Before we got to the nursery, I could hear him crying. Little stabs, shocking me like static electricity, went through my entire body as I approached the nursery. There all alone in the nursery was my baby boy, wailing at the top of his lungs, piercing my eardrums. My mother found the charge nurse and gave her a tongue lashing. After that, my baby came with all the other babies down the hall at feeding time. He was gently placed in my arms, and, triumphantly, I fed my baby boy for the first time.

Up until this point, my father had very little to say to me. Though no heated words had been exchanged in ages, his anger was still deafening. Several days after giving birth to my precious baby, my father came to me and said, "Rikki, Jeremy is your responsibility. You see to it that he is provided for and loved all the days of his life."

It didn't take long to realize my father was going to make it his responsibility to care for Jeremy. One look into Dad's eyes showed me my son was to be loved dearly. I began to understand redeeming love because my father accepted me back into his good graces regardless of my past indiscretions. He would love my baby because he loved me. I was beginning to understand the term "redeeming love." Thank you, Jesus.

We came home from the hospital to live with my parents. That first night at home with the new baby was nearly catastrophic. The baby was crying, and I was crying because I didn't know what was wrong. Mother was trying to console both of us because she checked on us periodically, telling me "Everything is fine; just change his diaper."

Every time she came into the room, he would stop crying. The minute she left the room, the wailing started up again. It is spooky how a tiny little creature makes such screeching, howling, ear-curling peals of "Pick me up now!" How can something so small and delicate rock the walls and shatter windows like an earthquake? Babies ought to coo and sigh contentedly instead of raising the hairs on the back of Mom's neck. What a nightmare!

Later that first night, my dad walked into the nursery. I couldn't contain my tears, and I fell into his arms, pleading, "Daddy, I don't know what to do. He won't stop screaming."

My dad reassuringly scooped my baby up and asked, "How often do you feed him?" I told him the nurse told me to feed him every four hours. He smiled, gazing down at Jeremy, "Really? Do you remember how often you were eating when you were carrying him in your tummy? Well, maybe he wants to eat a little sooner than every four hours." How true. My father saved the rest of the night. I fed Jeremy every two hours, and he slept! Thank you, Jesus, for mommies and daddies.

Things began to smooth out for Jeremy and me since we were living under the protection and guidance of my folks. After two months, it was time for me to assume responsibility for my son, as well as for myself. I went back to work and registered at a local college for two nights each week. This was a huge transition for me and my entire family. I would drop the baby off with a sitter, and my dad would pick him up and care for him until I could get home. This was a grueling process because I was tired from lack of sleep, but I persevered, remembering my dad's comment about Jeremy being my responsibility. I didn't want to let my son down, and I didn't want to let my father down again, especially after being accepted back into his good graces.

Dad became a loving, doting grandfather in caring for my son. One time when he picked him up at the sitter's, Jeremy was sitting in the middle of the floor, soaked and crying inconsolably. Reaching for his grandfather, his sobbing stopped, and my dad's heart was pierced by the thought of Jeremy being so neglected. Dad picked him up, wiped away the tears, and headed for the nearest ice cream parlor to pacify his terrifying day. After all, ice cream, even for an infant, always makes for a much better day!

Contemplating security for Jeremy's future, my father started a daycare at his church. He hired my grandmother, my sister, and my cousins to staff the daycare. How lucky for my baby and for me to have the best loving care as we fumbled forward, settling into our new roles as mother and son. Being my mother's first grandson and my father's favorite, Jeremy flourished. My folks delighted in spoiling him.

Starting to walk early at eight months, this precious bundle turned into a toddler, running all over the place. He wore all of us out. I never knew such energy could be contained in one little package. One day my mom and I went shopping at the mall. Jeremy got tired of walking, threw himself down on the floor, and threw a temper tantrum. I simply walked over him and kept going. Mother followed suit, and, in an instant, Jeremy was up and running to catch up. We had a good laugh, but he learned it was easier to ride in a stroller during shopping than to walk and get left behind.

Around the age of one, Jeremy got really sick. After taking him to the doctor, I started him on the prescribed dose of penicillin. Within minutes of that first dose, he began to wheeze and choke. He had an allergic reaction that scared me to death. Fortunately, my grandmother was there at the house and knew what was happening. She immediately gave him Benadryl, and the wheezing stopped. After thinking about what could have happened to my baby, I began to trust fewer people for his care.

Of course, sometimes my protectiveness went a little overboard, according to my family and friends. For example, one Christmas I bought a tricycle for him. He was so excited to get out and learn to ride it with my dad and little brother. I was the Grinch, making him wear knee pads and elbow pads over his already bulky coat. You could hear the groans all over the neighborhood, "Oh, Rikki, let that boy be a boy!"

Jeremy was nicknamed "Jabbo" by my play-sister's baby. Most of the time everyone called him by his nickname until he went to high school and thought it was too babyish.

Now Jabbo loved church. He was there every Sunday shadowing my father. I remembered one Sunday, Jabbo decided to dress for church without help from anyone. Proudly, he strutted out before the family in his favorite suit, which was two sizes too small; different colored socks; and his hair slicked back on the sides, parted crooked on the top. He loved his "Sunday-go-meeting" look, declaring, "This is how Grandpa dresses so he can preach our souls saved." Of course everyone had a good laugh except for me. I was furious with my father for allowing my son to look like a clown. Jabbo was most pleased with his preacher attire, and he ran down through the neighborhood, knocking on doors and telling all his playmates to come to church and praise the Lord. What a sight. He drew an army of little Christian soldiers and led them down the sidewalk all the way to church with his proud grandfather bringing up the rear, grinning from ear to ear. Thank you, sweet Jesus, for a precious memory savored in my heart for all eternity.

Strangely, my son and I did not sing much together when he was little. Listening to the radio, we might sing along with whatever song was playing at the time. We would laugh because many times we would break into song at the same time. Singing together was loud, and we were often moved to hand-clapping and foot-stomping.

I do remember seeing Jabbo sitting out in the congregation on Sundays. My son and I, along with the entire congregation, were moved when my father preached the gospel. He preached slowly and softly about the love of God. Then, picking up the tempo, he moved into the very goodness of God. Galloping down the homestretch, he ramped up the volume to conclude with redemption by the blood of Jesus. By the time he finished preaching, the choir would start crooning to old gospel favorites. I could look out at Jabbo and see your spirit was raising him up. He would sway with the music and sing his little heart out. Now, Lord, you gave me a voice that can easily be heard, but I swear that boy of mine could sing out too! He was singing to me; I was singing back to him; and my father, Reverend McNeil, was caught between the two of us, resonating with his tenor voice. Together, we rocked many a Sunday with our favorite anthem:

Where do I go when there's nobody else
to turn to?
Who do I talk to when nobody wants to listen?
I go to the Rock
I know He's able.
I go to the Rock

Lord, I still sing this song today, and I love it. I believe my son and father are singing along with me, rocking in the arms of your Holy Spirit. You are my Rock!

Jeremy was baptized as a child in my father's church by my father. Now that's special! My son loved the church, and he loved you, his Lord. Hear my prayer, O Lord, as I humbly offer you my prayers of thanksgiving. Thank you for my precious boy—a gift I treasured and delighted in for twenty-three years.

Sweet Hour 3
Prayers for the Village

As is true with many children today, it takes a village" to raise kids. Too many young fathers turn their backs on their babies. Babies grow up without a sense of identity, not to mention struggling for the basic necessities because many fathers deny their God-given responsibilities. Lord, protect our babies who grow up without fathers.

Though Jeremy did not have a traditional intact family, I believe he was nurtured and guided by a loving, close-knit village. I have to give lots of credit to my father, mother, and grandmother. They offered tender loving care in providing for all my baby's needs while I worked and went to school. All through kindergarten and elementary school, my folks watched over Jabbo, took him to church, worked on school projects, read books, or took him to the ranch for fun days around the animals.

My grandmother inspired his love for home cooking He was often found in the kitchen helping his GeeGee stir up her famous lemon pie or licking the beaters from the cream cake, which was his number-one requested birthday cake. No matter what she cooked, Jabbo—and all of us-loved and devoured her cuisine.

My grandmother also had a way of cooking up activities, which I sometimes was not aware of, for her grandson. For example, she signed him up for swimming lessons without my consent, and he won a trophy. She let him try out for football and basketball without my consent also. Oh my, he was a terrific basketball player. He wanted to join a gospel singing group, and GeeGee encouraged him, knowing I had already said, "No way!" Sometimes after school, she'd clap her hands and watch him perform song and dance routines during home recitals of which she was the only audience.

Mommy and Gee Gee played dominoes for hours with Jabbo to help build up his math skills. He loved school, especially math and science. My mother, a teacher, was thrilled with his progress at school. She thought he was the world's brightest student. I could not have asked for better tutors.

I was afraid for Jabbo much of his life. I can't explain it, but, in the back of my mind, the fear persisted. I rationalized that if he didn't involve himself in sports, he wouldn't get hurt. If he didn't play with other kids, he wouldn't get his feelings hurt. Much of my mothering was described by "No, son, you can't. It's too dangerous. You might get hurt. No, son, not today."

I preferred giving him all the clothes, all the toys, and all the very best I could buy. Sometimes the best is not always what we think it is. I worked hard to provide him with things that don't last, things that don't even hold memories.

It was strange that Jeremy told many people I was his hero, but, looking back, it was my family who were the heroes. My father taught him to love the Lord. My mommy encouraged him to appreciate the learning process and excel in school. My grandmother challenged him to discover his passions. Lord, I don't think I inspired my son. Why he would call me his hero, I don't know. Maybe I should have prayed for his protection instead of trying to be his guard.

Jeremy did not have a relationship with his own father. Truly, it would not have been a stable environment nor beneficial had his father been in the picture I did not encourage Jeremy to seek out a relationship with his father. He seldom asked about Alvin.

God, I can't help but wonder if I had followed your plan for my life earlier, if I had loved Jeremy's father, if I had not been so young, so unprepared for all of life's responsibilities-if, if, if only—would Jeremy's life have turned out differently? Would he be alive today?

There were many times I felt inadequate as a mom. Also, I admit reluctantly that my feelings were hurt finding out he would rather live with his grandmother than with me at times. How was I to compete with her? My best meal was a can of spaghetti with wieners and lots of cheese on top.

I admit I was jealous when my mother took him to school. She would meet with the teachers at open house. She never missed school programs or field days. I'm sure he preferred her coming to the school events instead of me. I often felt a rivalry with my mom for my son's affections. Maybe that's why I spoiled him with things.

I'll never forget when I gave him a hundred dollars to put his school clothes in layaway. Instead, he came out with two shirts from Neiman Marcus. My grandmother chastised me, saying, "Like mother, like son." For as long as I can remember, I worked two jobs to give him the best things in life. Lord, I should have prayed for him. That would have been best.

Until the age of twelve, Jabbo's life fared pretty well in our little "family village." The family influence was moral, ethical, and spiritual. The village expanded to include a wonderful group of boys who spent more time together than apart. They were Reuben, Scot, Mario, and Randall along with Phillip and Jerry, who were cousins. It was Jabbo who captained this crew. All were good boys, well behaved, and polite. I often remarked on my son's good fortune of having good friends. Especially as I looked from the choir loft on those boys bowing their heads and praying together in the church pew; I was thrilled.

I hoped our village laid a sturdy enough foundation to weather through Jeremy's entire life, but, truthfully, I never gave it much thought. After all, I was busy working, planning for financial security, and I was involved in one bad relationship after another. I was in the middle of my life, and sometimes living my life left little time for building up my son's foundation. I guess that was why I did not notice the subtle changes, like his newfound sassy mouth and attitude or his sudden interest in girls. I should have paid better attention. I should have prayed harder.

Somewhere between middle school and high school, things changed dramatically. Now he was still a good kid, made good grades, and I was very proud. I believed good grades were the best indicator for "He's okay. No problem." Sporting his independence, curfews were missed, his attire looked kind of funky, and he hung out with different kids. He seemed drawn to one girl in particular, though she was younger and jealous of other girls.

He remained tenderhearted, usually kind and respectful to his grandmother and me. He continued to come to church on occasion, though he lost interest. He told me he had problems with the church and was disillusioned by hypocrites. But when I sang at church, Jeremy almost always delighted me with his presence. What a joy for me to look out in the congregation and see him proudly swaying and singing along with me. His heart was in the right place with motives crystal clear as a mountain stream, but his judgment was fogged up already with poor choices.

Never having a relationship with his own father, Jabbo rejected the men in my life. He only knew William and Oscar because I was married to them. He despised them both, especially Oscar. He refused to live with us, and I did not argue, because the men in my life were simply not good role models. In the back of my mind, I never wanted them in my son's life, fearing one of them would hurt him. Since my father was no longer alive, good male influences were lacking during his adolescent years.

Now he was plenty loved by his grandmothers and me, but we were not necessarily strong, consistent boundary makers. Again, my life involved work, church, and bad marriages. Consequently, my relationship with Jeremy suffered, and our lives felt a little disconnected at times. The majority of the time, he lived with my grandmother. Often, when I picked him up for weekend stays at my apartment, I would see the saddest look in his eyes as he waved goodbye to Gee-Gee. Since I didn't know for sure what he was thinking, my heart broke sensing his reluctance to come. I felt I was not doing a very good job as his mother. Was I the weakest link in the village? O God, I should have prayed for our village.

The City had no need of the sun or of the moon to shine in it for the glory of God illuminated it. The Lamb is its light. But there shall by no means enter it anything that defiles, or causes an abomination or a lie...

Revelation 21:23, 27

Sweet Hour 4
Prayers for Protection against Evil

In high school, Jeremy's safe and protective village was pillaged by the drug world. The drug world was deeply entrenched in our neighborhood long before Jeremy was born. Growing up in the neighborhood, I never really paid any mind to drugs. My family and I coexisted in this drug-infested culture, and it spread like a deadly virus, festering beyond our village into neighboring communities, cities, and nations.

You see, God, in South Dallas, just like any other village in the world, illegal drugs were and still are as common as the corner grocery store. Illegal drugs were and still remain the most lucrative form of commerce anywhere. In this enterprise of illegal drugs, the CEOs may be our outstanding, respected, and honored leaders of our communities. The executive sales representatives are the best of our young men. They are the husbands and fathers who probably hold down legitimate jobs on the side. Next in the ranks are the distributors who "run" or deliver the goods to the paying customers and our resident junkies. They buy quick fixes with money generated from petty thefts or muggings. The drug world is structured like any cartel that is syndicated to generate revenues and control expenses. It is a very big business worldwide, and it profits more money and provides more employment opportunities than most other major businesses in the world combined. Just as General Motors was the largest employer of Detroit in its heyday and everyone was somehow connected or knew someone who was employed by GM, either through direct employment or outside contracts, so goes the drug business. It was and still is Satan's largest corporation located in the midst of our village. O God, protect us from this evil.

Knowing now how evil sweeps through a community like the Black Plague, I now realize how vital it is for our communities to surrender to the blood of Christ to save us from the destruction of drugs. We need to bathe in your blood, paint it over our front doors, spray a protective coating on our children, and pray for your blood to rain over our villages. Lord Jesus, you are the only way to cleanse the villages in our world of illegal drugs. Your business is big enough to conquer this evil generating corporation. Victory in Jesus!

> I know it was the blood,
> One day when I was lost,
> He died upon that cross.
> I know it was the blood for me.

The lure of fast money is hard to compete against. The "men" in our neighborhood paraded around in Mercedes-Benzes. They flaunted expensive clothes and wore gold around their necks with diamonds on their fingers. They went to the Cowboys and Mavericks games. Wow! Just like the rich and the famous. However, the flashing decadence sometimes reversed, as these same "men" were seen buying raffles for charity or funding a church's project to feed the poor. Evil can be so attractive, look so caring, so righteous, and most people won't look a gift horse in the mouth. I talked until I was blue about easy money to Jeremy. I tried to set a good example of working hard, saving for something special, and self-respect, all the things I remembered my mommy and father tried to tell me. I went to church. I sang praises to you, the Lord. What else was I to do? I should have been a better example. I should have prayed to be a better competitor.

Jeremy had a good heart, which made him an easy prey. He wanted to help me get started in a recording career. He dreamed of opening his own restaurant someday. His heart strings tugged at him to help people who were in need. While in high school, he started to prepare and plan for these dreams. He worked parttime jobs, trying to figure out a way to make his dreams happen. I stressed the importance of education and hard work over and over. I thought we were on the same page

Graduation day came, and I was filled with pride and joy. Jeremy graduated with honors. As he crossed that stage, I felt proud along with a sense of relieve. "Whew! My boy beat the odds. Now if I can get him through college, we will have a home run!"

Following graduation, he went to a culinary school and trained with a prestigious chef in Dallas. He was serious about learning culinary arts. I remember one day he called me at work crying because a girl in his class had stolen his recipe, and his teacher did nothing about it. What mother doesn't try to fix the problem for her baby? Outraged by the teacher's actions, that's exactly what I did. I left work to give his teacher a piece of my mind, which resulted in Jabbo's utter embarrassment. Awkwardly, we managed to move on from that fiasco to another in a short time.

Jabbo was a gifted chef and was awarded a scholarship to a culinary institute in New York City. God, I should have jumped for joy; instead, I blocked his path toward his dream. All I could think about was my baby being all by himself in New York and far away from me. I was too scared to let him go. I wasn't ready for my baby to leave my arms. Was I concerned for his safety? Yes. Was I worried about myself? Yes. So I nixed his plans. I stood in his way and helped determine a different path for my baby. Why didn't I pray first?

Hoping to change the direction, I convinced Jeremy to enroll in a community college. He was very angry with me, yet he still wanted to please me, just like I wanted to please my father. With his new mantle of sadness, my son drifted into the sea of the lost while I went back to my life of work, church, and bad relationships. I knew our surroundings. I knew about fast money, but surely Jabbo was raised right. No worries. I would work hard to pay for college, and he would be okay. I did not want to see it any other way. Lord, I should have paid more attention.

The dealers, they paid attention--plenty of attention! They were aware of his dreams, desires, and needs. Part of their lure was to wait patiently for Jeremy to recognize he could have it all. The waiting was not long. Just as Satan tempted your Son, Jesus, for forty days in the desert, so too he lured my boy. Satan declared, "If you worship me, it will all be yours" (Luke 4:7). Going into the drug business does not require an education, nor does it value the higher standards of good morals. It is the path of least resistance, and the only prerequisite is the handing over of the soul. Jeremy was ripe for the picking

Sweet Hour 5
Prayer for Deliverance

I was told my son was committed to finding a way into the drug business as early as high school. After starting classes in college, he pursued this venture quickly and passionately. The boy was on a mission. He sought out contracts among the fast moneymakers. Hearing the rumors of Jeremy's drug pursuits on the street, my brother threatened the dealers in the south to steer clear of my son. My little brother told me, when it was too late, that he pleaded with Jeremy by citing the dangers of being connected, but my son paid no heed. After all, the young men in our neighborhood who sold illegal drugs made more money in a day's time than he could make in a month at his part-time jobs.

Why did my brother not come to me and tell me what was happening back then? If I had known, what difference would it have made? There was always someone else around every corner telling my son something different. As things rapidly changed, I really didn't know what to think. In my heart, I knew things were not right, but it was easier to deny than to acknowledge. No mother wants to think the worst of their child. Regardless of my hesitancy or my brother's efforts to dissuade Jeremy from entering the drug profession, he was not swayed from his course. He was determined to make a lot of money as fast as possible and then get out. He had to make enough to fund my first CD of gospel music, and he wanted to open his own restaurant. Besides, there were other needs to be tended to. In no time, he was selling drugs.

Jeremy moved up the corporate ladder quickly. The men he approached for a job were soon working for him. I was not aware of his business acumen, but I noticed plenty of other things. My son and I started having problems.

I was devastated to learn he quit college, and we argued about the company he was keeping. I started getting calls from the police department. One time he was pulled over for a traffic violation, and money was found in the trunk. He was not arrested; however, he refused to tell me where the money came from, which provoked another argument. He informed me that "This is not your concern. Stay out of my business."

From then on, Jeremy built a barrier around himself. He only opened the gates periodically, allowing me in for special moments not to keep me out of his life but to protect me. Was I aware? Probably, but again, it was easier to accept his closed gates than to acknowledge the secrets behind his wall.

Part of protecting me from the truth of Jabbo's new path, I found out so many years later, was the secret involvement of other family members. My brother, who supposedly had tried to keep him out of the drug business, told me he protected Jabbo by being his money handler. They partnered up to ensure no connection between Jeremy and the money from illegal transactions that were made. Lord, I'm not quite sure what that meant, but I think my brother wanted me to think he had my son's back while he too was connected to the drug business.

Not only was my brother involved, my sister was too. She had been using drugs for years, but somehow she was connected to my son's newfound business venture. How could my own family have known and been involved with Jeremy in his illegal endeavors, and why? Secrets! How could they encourage him and tell him to keep these evil, life-crushing secrets from me? God, were they really trying to protect me? Why did I allow protection? Why does fear keep us from seeing the truth? Why didn't I do something? Why did I look the other way? Lord, hear my prayers and deliver me from these agonizing questions.

Then they cried out to the Lord in their trouble, and He delivered them out of their distresses.

(Psalm 107:6)

By the age of twenty, Jeremy was deeply connected in the drug world. He moved in with his girlfriend, Ruby, and her mother. I am almost certain that he paid the rent and provided the groceries. He bought a car and put the title in my name. Money flowed abundantly. He spent it helping others, but he also spent it foolishly Jabbo always loved jewelry, and he sported some beautiful pieces. He loved quality clothes--that was my fault, because I did too-and paid for expensive, tailored shirts. He wore his newfound prosperity proudly.

His good friends-Paul, John, and Mark—were on drugs and also connected to the business as Jeremy's bodyguards. It wasn't long before each was arrested and sent to prison. I think Jeremy must have seen something special in Reuben and another childhood friend named Scott. He steered them another direction. He swore to those boys, "If I ever see you go near the drug lords for drugs or dealing, I swear I'll come after you, and then I will go after the dealers." To this day, thank you, Lord Jesus, those boys are safely walking on your path. That's why it was so hard to believe the bad things said about my son. I believed my son would have given the shirt off his back to anyone who needed it. He considered the lives of his good friends too worthy to risk the lifestyle he chose for himself.

Drugs and alcohol were part of Jeremy's and Ruby's lifestyle. Their relationship was always in turmoil.

Ruby announced several pregnancies, usually when my son tried to break up with her, yet I never saw a baby. People told me Ruby and her mother would often steal from Jeremy when he was passed out from drinking too much. This side of Jabbo was an ugly sight. He was falling further and further into a world out of control. This was hard for me to watch, and sometimes I chose not to see.

When Ruby got pregnant, he came to me and cried, "What am I going to do?"

I told him the same thing my father told me: "Marry her and provide for your baby." I further told him he had to get his life together because he now had a more important responsibility. I told him you, God, required him to set a good example through righteous living.

Fleetingly, I thought the pregnancy may be a good thing for him, a reason for him to change his life. He could go back to school and work a legitimate job. I encouraged him to talk to our pastor, my godfather, and he did. They had a good conversation, and I think Jeremy wanted to make things better so he could be a good father.

He asked Ruby to marry him and presented her with a beautiful engagement ring. O Lord, he didn't want me to feel slighted, so he bought me a beautiful ring and presented it to me on the same day. His heart was filled with love for me, for his fiancée, and for his baby on the way. He was going to make things right. My heart was beating with hope! Again, his intentions were right, but his judgment remained skewed. The proverbial "get back on the right foot" never got a chance to begin.

We seldom got together for visits anymore, but one night my son was at my house. It was one of those rare and delightful moments when I easily recognized my little boy, carefree from the chains of chaos he normally wore. I talked about my job and threw out little hints about going back to school. He prepared a delicious dish. We sampled everything before finally sitting down at the table to delicately devour our delectable meal. How we enjoyed ourselves. That evening was one of those shared moments only a mother can treasure. We were laughing when the phone rang, disrupting our evening. It's funny how things can change in the blink of an eye. Answering the phone, he was visibly shaken as we learned someone had broken into his apartment.

Jeremy frantically demanded, "Rich, take me home!" All the way there, he was screaming, "How could she do this? Oh my God, how could she do this? What am I going to do?"

"Do what, Jabbo? Who, Ruby? What has she done?" I cried, hurting for my baby. "Calm down. Wait until we get there and see what has happened."

"She stole money that does not belong to me. This is going to get me killed," he anguished.

What was I to do? No matter what, my words were wasted and useless. O Lord, to say I felt helpless is an understatement. At that moment, I had paid attention. There was clarity, and it was loud and clear. There was no denial this time. My son was deeply entrenched in drug dealing.

I didn't know how deep until years later. The sad part was, nearly everyone, including many of my family members, not only knew his involvement, but they were connected in business with him.

Looking back, I remembered preaching to my son, "Stay in school. Get your act together. Stop hanging around those thugs who mean you no good." All the while, Satan proclaimed louder, "Oh, you know how your mother is, Miss Christian Goody-Goody. She's just forgotten what it's like to be young. Go on and live in the fast lane while you can. It's fun! Be happy. What does she know?"

I was told later Ruby was the person who had stolen the money. From what I gathered, it was a huge sum of money. My son and I never spoke about this incident after that night. In my heart, I fretted and feared for him choosing a life in the drug world. I worried about prison and addiction. I even worried about what other people would think.

I plotted to take him out of the business, move far away, and start over again. I pleaded with you, God. My prayers bargained for the life of my son. "If only you will save my boy, I promise to change my life. I'll be better. I'll go to church every day. I'll help the widows. I'll feed the poor. Whatever you want, God, tell me, and I'll do it. Anything at all, I promise. Please just save him. Deliver my boy from this oppressive enemy."

The Lord will preserve him and keep him alive, and he will be blessed on the earth; You will not deliver him to the will of his enemies.

Psalm 41:2

Sweet Hour 6
Prayers for Justice

Often, late at night, the phone would ring and wake me from my already restless sleep. Sometimes it was hangups; other times it was the police. I dreaded nights by now. One night the call came from Jeremy. He had been arrested. He told me he had been a passenger in the back seat of his friend's car. They had been pulled over by the police for an expired license tag. The police asked them to step out of the car, both complied. My son told me he wasn't driving. The police were talking to his friend, the driver, and they examined the driver's license. Jeremy decided to walk across the street and get something to eat and drink. He thought it was okay to walk over to the convenience store since the police were ticketing the driver. As he began to walk away, the police officer ordered my son to stop. He handcuffed him and arrested him for resisting arrest.

My son swore there was no reason for the police to even question him. After all, it wasn't his car. Not only did they question him, they searched him and found nothing on him. Taking him to the police station to book him on charges of resisting arrest and disorderly conduct, one of the officers noticed Jabbo fidgeting in the backseat of the patrol car. Arriving at the station, the officer searched the backseat and found drugs between the seats, so it was told by the police officer.

I was leery of Jabbo's story. It sounded contrived, but still, I wanted to believe him. The rest of the night, I paced the floor torn between anger and fear. The next morning, charges were filed. I asked questions over and over. I wondered how could anyone with handcuffs on reach into a back pocket and hide drugs between the seats. The police never addressed this matter to my satisfaction

For three months, I went with my son to court. We would sit all day, only to be rescheduled for another date because either the attorney or arresting officer would not show. I grew impatient with the court system. Where was the lawyer, and who hired him? My son dismissed my questions, telling me he was his friend's attorney. After meeting with the attorney, I was terribly troubled and perplexed. He advised my son to plead guilty. He assured us this was the easiest and fastest way to get him out of jail. Stunned, I walked out into a hallway, not knowing what to do.

Again, the feeling of inadequacy flooded through me. Could the lawyer be trusted? Did I trust my own son? I wanted to trust him. What was I to do? This was my only son, who I adored. He swore to me he was not guilty. O Lord, I prayed for justice.

Therefore the Lord will wait, that He may be gracious to you, and therefore He will be exalted, that He may have mercy on you. For the Lord is a God of justice; blessed are all those who wait for Him.

Isaiah 30:18

Entering the courtroom for the plea hearing was surreal. My son and I walked to our seats. We both were trembling. Nervously, we sat down to await his fate. Facing before the judge, my son slowly stood up. The judge asked, "How do you plead?"

Jeremy's knees buckled as he turned toward me and cried out, "Rich, I'm not guilty. I can't do this." My heart sank, and I reached out to hold my baby. This was a gut-wrenching display of raw emotion. I knew he was telling the truth. My motherly instinct lashed out to fiercely protect my son at all costs.

I pleaded with the judge, "Can't you see he is not guilty? God, help us!" The judge banged his gavel to gain control. Amazingly, he barked at Jeremy's lawyer to step forward. In a loud voice, the judge suggested the lawyer exit his courtroom and make a better effort on behalf of his client before entering the plea again. Before clearing the courtroom, he ordered the plea hearing to be rescheduled.

Had I heard chastisement in his voice? Yes, and I marched out of the courtroom ahead of my son filled with new resolve. The lawyer followed, shaking his head discourteously. I stood up to him, face-to-face, and told him we no longer required his services. He reeked of alcohol.

Desiring to be my son's hero, I was determined to get him help before the next hearing. I turned to my pastor and godfather, Pastor McNealy. Trustingly, I laid everything out before him. He agreed to help us however he could. I thought maybe he would be a character witness for Jeremy, but he did so much more. Before the hearing began, he found an opportunity to visit with the arresting officer. Pastor McNealy asked the officer to explain again how it was possible for the drugs to have been stashed between the seats while the accused was handcuffed, especially since Jeremy had already been searched before he was ever put in the patrol car.

It was time. We were directed into the courtroom. No sooner had we sat down, the charges against my son were dismissed. He was freed. I can't explain what happened, other than it was you, O God, with help from Pastor McNealy, who stepped in and armed us with justice. Thank you, Jesus!

If it had not been for the Lord on my side Where would I be? Where would I be?

PART 4

Trials and Tribulations

How I loved my boy. We had a terrible argument. Anger was building, and our tempers flared with each other. I kept shouting, "You're going to ruin your life hanging out with those creeps. They are no good! Don't you know they're just using you?"

Shaking his head at me in disgust, he shouted back, "Nothing will ever make you happy!" These were the last words I ever heard my son say.

I remembered these words, harsh and condemning, as I walked out of the county morgue on the night of January 31, 1995—the night my son was murdered. I begged to see my son, but the staff refused to let me see him. He was already being prepped for an autopsy. Randall, the funeral director, who was a family friend, had been called, and he was there at the morgue to meet me. He was able to get a photo of my son laid out on a slab. I didn't recognize Jeremy in the picture. I refused to believe it was him. I never got to hold my baby in my arms. All I had was a black-and-white snapshot, and I didn't even get to hold that for long. Someone took the photo from me, saying it was for the records. The world fainted away from me.

There are many thoughts on trials and tribulations. Some dictionaries define the word trial using the synonym of affliction. Affliction is the subjection of suffering. Suffering means "to feel pain or distress." Tribulation can be defined as "a grievous trial or experience, an affliction or trouble." Basically, trials and tribulations are terms for human pain and suffering.

Christianity often attributes trials and tribulations as tests for one's endurance, character building, patience, and, most importantly, faith. Now, Father God, I know it's not you who inflicts pain and suffering, nor do you write out the exams to test us. Rather, my faith tells me to trust you in the midst of my suffering because you have overcome the world.

My trials and tribulations did not start with the death of my son, but I can truthfully say his murder was the height of my suffering and the longest test of my life to date. Though scriptures point to the results of trials and tribulations as positive, life-enhancing benefits, it never crossed my mind that I would gain anything in the midst of my suffering.

In 2 Corinthians 1:8-10, Paul talked about being under great pressure far beyond his ability to endure, despairing even life, but encouraged us to set our hope on God. After all, Paul reminded us that Christ overcame death and delivered us, and he will continue to deliver us. Though I went through my trials and tribulations because there was no other choice, I know now the result was life changing.

We are bound for the Promised Land.
No more trials... Don't you want to go? No more tribulations... Don't you want to go?
No more sickness... Don't you want to go?
No more heartache... Don't you want to go?
For we are bound, we are bound for the
Promised Land.

Oh, but, dear Lord, I had a long way to go before considering the benefits to my trials and tribulations. My son was murdered. I was not interested in character building. There was no gain, only loss. I lost all hope.

The Shock of Trials and Tribulations

Children aren't supposed to die and leave their parents behind. Nature's natural course determines the parent dies first, and then the child becomes the heir to reign in his parent's stead, thus securing his own future, hopes, and dreams. If the child dies first, there is no future, no hopes, and no dreams.

After leaving the morgue, I was whisked away to my grandmother's home. As we turned the corner to her house, most of the gawkers were gone. A few police remained at my son's death scene. The blazing strobe lights on most of the patrol cars had been turned off. Crime scene tape had cornered off the area. Slowly passing by, I stared out the car window, looking, wondering what had happened there. I had no clue what it was I expected to see. I forced myself to look straight ahead as though I could will away this horrible scene of death and destruction.

Pulling into the driveway at Gee-Gee's house, people were everywhere-wandering about, going in and out of the house, sitting on the front porch-waiting for us. I'm sure they were loved ones family, friends, or neighbors. For the life of me, I didn't recognize their faces. It was eerie, no faces. Someone opened my door to help me out. That was the first face I recognized. It was Mr. Panama Jack. He helped me into the house and led me through the living room. I collapsed into the arms of my mother and grandmother.

I wept, not really understanding why, but I sensed something dreadful, something vile, and something horrific was happening to me. I physically felt a sickening assault in my gut, yet I could not reconcile what or who had stabbed me. My mother stroked my head, comforting me, and gently, she dabbed at the cascade of tears. I felt my mommy's warm tears drop down next to mine. With our sorrow pouring out, our tears flowed together in a stream down my cheek. We wept together.

Confusion quieted down in the room as my mother told her story. You see, God, my mother walked down to that corner of death and identified my son's body lying facedown in an alleyway. She hoped her words would console me. She relayed to me that his hands were in a praying position. Later on, I remembered her words. I replayed them over and over in my mind so my soul might be comforted. I kept visualizing my son in conversation right at the moment of his death, with his hands seeking forgiveness from God. He must have been praying for your comfort and strength for me. Longing to know my son was with you in heaven, O Lord, those words my mother gave me were my only assurance I had for Jeremy's salvation. He died with his hands folded in prayer.

The rest of the night was a blur. People would come in and hug me. Some would say, "It's God's will." I heard moans, intermittent wails, and whispers. I was sure people were saying, or perhaps I invented, "She can sing and save everyone, but not her own son." Those words haunted me over and over.

There was random confusion. My attention was directed and redirected from one person to another. At times I truly felt the room spinning with people circling the room, and I heard bits and pieces of conversations about the terrible tragedy." One well-meaning friend came up to me and said I needed to call Jeremy's father. Another handed me the phone. It rang several times. Alvin answered, and I told him his son was dead, straight out. I didn't know what else to say. Silence filled the airwaves, and I don't remember if he said anything or not. It didn't matter. I hung up the phone.

A short time later, Jeremy's father was there, weaving his way through all the folks until he saw me. Attempting to offer comfort, his words of consolation were "Rikki, we have to be strong because there are other children to think of." The absurdity of those words enraged me. He had other children, but I only had Jeremy. How dare him. I wanted to slap this man who seldom even acknowledged my boy. Opening my mouth to scream out, someone tugged at my elbow. It was Panama Jack. He held out my coat and said, "Rikki, we need to go and get you some rest."

I have so little memory of that night after learning about Jabbo's death. Panama Jack managed to get me home, bathe off the filth from the morgue, and put me to bed. I didn't want to sleep. I wanted to die.

Most of those first darkened hours of sleeplessness, I replayed all the details I could remember. I wanted to figure out how I could change what happened. I wanted to erase and rewrite the nightmare that screeched through my thoughts. I could not erase the scene of my boy laid out on a slab. That hideous picture appeared and reappeared on the chalkboards of my mind. Jerking up out of bed, I clutched at my chest and tried to catch my breath. Struggling to breathe, I took several deep breaths to stop the suffocating. How absurd! Why would I care about breathing? If the breaths stopped, the nightmare would end. I held my breath, praying for suffocation. It did not come. The breaths kept gasping, and I kept clutching my chest. There was no erasing the memories. My mind dredged up every detail of the night and the circumstances leading up to it. Fighting the panic, I begged to you, O God, "Please wash my thoughts, turn off my brain, grant me peace, and let me erase this nightmare."

"Nothing will ever make you happy," I heard Jabbo's voice yell at me over and over.

The panic consumed me all night. Tearing at my soaked gown, I implored, "God, I can't do this! Take me away. Take me to my son. I want to go with him. Let me die."

I wrestled with you, O God, until early morning, when I felt Panama Jack rocking me. He combed through my hair with strong but gentle fingers, trying to smooth out the tangles from the turbulent night. I didn't recognize his comforting care or his sad eyes tearing up with pity. My heart and mind were at war. There was no consolation.

My mother and my grandmother were ill from grief. They were unable to go with me to make arrangements the next morning. They sent me with some insurance papers and told me my older half-brother would meet me at the funeral home to help me instead.

The planning was interrupted numerous times at the funeral home while my brother answered one call after another. He excused himself from the room, citing the call as "business." I overheard him setting up tee times for golf! Before we went into the scary room to pick out my son's casket, another business call came. My brother left me to take the call.

Alone with my thoughts, I remembered asking my brother many times to talk with Jeremy about the bad crowd he was running with, but that never happened. I also remembered asking my pastor to counsel with him, and he did, but by the time he did talk with Jabbo, it was too late. I blamed myself for not getting help for him sooner, but I was afraid of what my pastor and others would think about my son. Looking back, I asked myself, why would I care what others thought? When you love a child and you know they are in trouble, it doesn't matter what others think. I should have searched the world for help.

Going into the casket room, I felt pressure weighing me down. My legs weakened, barely able to hold me up. God, I had to get out of that room. The absurdity of shopping for a casket made me sick.

Further absurdity caused my skin to crawl as we traipsed across the cemetery to pick out the plot. We rode around and looked at a dozen sites. The funeral director, my brother, and I bantered back and forth. "This one has a great view." "That one doesn't get morning light." "This one is too far away, but it does have a nice statue of Mary close by." "That one has trees blocking the view. "God, why was I there, and why did I have to pick out a place where my son's body would lay forever? My legs wobbled; my hands shook. I wanted to be anywhere except at my son's graveyard.

My best friend picked out my son's attire for his funeral much like I helped him pick out his tuxedo for the prom. As with most young men, Jeremy hated suits, so we shopped for a new shirt and tie, vest, and pants. He would look so handsome in his beautiful casket. Absurd!

Our family friend at the funeral home promised to fix the large abrasion on Jabbo's face before the services. He said it resulted from the fall as my son slid across the pavement. I thought he was trying to spare me from knowing it was from a bullet exiting his head. O God, I could not bear the thought of my baby's beautiful face being ravaged. Acid from the pit of my stomach rose up, burning my throat. My head pounded with each beat of my heart. Anxiety washed over me. God, take me out of this misery.

Going through these motions of absurdity, there was a strong disconnect with the reality that I was preparing to bury Jeremy. In between the motions, it occurred to me I was being punished. I knew judgment would come one day for all the wrongs I had done, but not like this, not now. Yet I felt responsible for my son's death. I should have paid more attention, been a better mother. I scarcely remembered anything else on my first day of no longer being a mother except I did not want to breathe any longer.

After the burial, people passed by to offer their sympathies and condolences. Many people stood in line. Some I knew, and others I had no idea. I saw his best friends, Reuben and Scott, standing in the line. As they made their way to me, each gently bowed their head, struggling to find the right words. No one knew what to say. As I reached toward them, Scott took one of my hands. He stood, patting and rubbing my hand. Reuben dropped to his knees in front of me, laid his head in my lap, and sobbed. I was strangely warmed by their display of love, and I wanted to comfort them both. I closed my eyes, remembering what it was like to touch my baby boy. They were alive, and I was glad. Hopefully my baby helped save their lives from the perils of drugs and early graves.

After the services, the first days without Jeremy were odd. Basically, I followed instructions from Mr. Panama, my mother, and grandmother. They managed the minutes, hours, and the days of my loss. It wasn't as if I trusted them or relied upon their guidance; I simply just did what they told me. It's hard to explain the robotic movements during such times.

Words cannot describe what living is like after losing your son. I was confused, bewildered. The loss was forever. No telling how long forever would last here on earth. I was burdened with the thought of living even one day without Jeremy. My aloneness alienated me from all others. I was alone with my sense of loss before the pain and suffering ever began.

I knew no rules, no guidelines or boundaries of time or space in my new journey of loss. There was no map. I had no energy to search for you, O Lord, to lead me through the wilderness of loss. I felt abandoned by you, my Savior. I was in a place I did not choose.

I wanted no part of participating in this horror. I panicked. I was shocked. I longed for the days before the murder.

Oh that I were as in months past, as in the days when God watched over me; when his lamp shone upon my head, and when by His light I walked through darkness; just as I was in the days of my prime, when the friendly counsel of God was over my tent; when the Almighty was yet with me, when my children were around me; when my steps were bathed with cream, and the rock poured out rivers of oil for me!

Job 29:2-6

The Questions

My journey into grief began. I did not know how long it would last. Would it be one year, five years, or fifteen years or my entire life? I hoped not. I didn't want to live one moment suffering the grief of Jeremy's death.

Between the "it's not true" and "this didn't happen," I tried to comprehend my dilemma of living in grief by sorting through the details. It was important to be methodical and thorough in putting the pieces together. The reconstruction of my son's murder broke through the starting gate with bounding questions, lots of questions.

Did he suffer? Was he aware? Did he bear the gunshots? What were his last thoughts? Did he think about me? Who was with him? Where was he going? Of all the questions I would probably never get the answers to, the most pressing and haunting question was: Why did this happen?

If I was ever to understand why, I had to find out how it happened. I began the task by asking all my family and friends if they had any knowledge or even theories about Jabbo's murder. I called on his friends and acquaintances. Some of Jabbo's friends wanted to help by hunting down the killers like vigilantes, wanting justice. Truthfully, the thought was appealing, but it was more pressing to know what had happened and why. It was interesting to note how people responded to me. At first they graciously offered kindness with comforting words and inquiries of "How can we help?" As soon as my questions began, they avoided answering me and quickly changed the subject. Sometimes while comforting me, various people recited their recollections of special things my son had done for them. I would go away thinking, If he was so good, why on earth would someone kill him?

Many friends and family members had good intentions. I'm sure they thought the proverbial "get over it" by not talking about the murder or Jabbo's death was the best thing for me. I sensed it was best for them. If no one talked about the tragedy, maybe it would disappear. They tried but were uncomfortable listening to me go over and over all the details and asking the same questions repeatedly. I felt people distance themselves from me and my tragedy. I began to resent them and their good intentions.

God, forgive me, but I was so mad at you. At night in bed, I would scream, "How could you let this happen?" And in the next moment: "Why didn't you save my baby?"

My anger kept me from crying. It even gave me a sense of being in control and having power. I thought it was better to build a wall around myself and not let you, God, or anyone else see what was really going on in my head. I was determined to put the pieces of the puzzle together by myself. I would get my answers!

I turned to the detectives; they had to answer my questions. They were the professionals, and I trusted them to help sort everything out for me. Instead of answering my questions, they protected me from the gruesome details. Initially, the police were forthcoming on the details, but a few weeks later it was, "We'll get back to you." A young female was one of many detectives assigned to the case. She learned that three men chased Jeremy across the street into an alley. She reported that he was shot six times from behind. Not wanting to see the autopsy report, I imagined he had been shot once in the head, twice in the legs, and three times in the back. This sounded like more than just a drug deal gone badly. How could anyone hate my child so much to execute him from behind?

I saw the young detective walk the streets around our neighborhood, asking questions. Most people didn't answer their doors, and those who did gave her very little information. She was kind and tried her best to be responsive to my questions.

After more than three months, I decided things were not going anywhere fast enough to suit me. I wanted my son's murder solved. By now, calls to the police department were seldom returned. When the calls were answered, I would get a message saying, "We will call you if anything further develops or if there is something to report." I felt the police were not showing enough interest because maybe they thought my son was one less drug dealer in the world. My frustration was brewing, and I took things into my hands to further the investigation along. I walked down Oakland Avenue and put up posters offering a reward of $1,000 for information leading to an arrest. By the time I walked an entire block posting the reward, got in my car, and drove back down the block to go home, all the posters had been taken down. I was furious! Why would anyone take the posters down? Hearing this, my mother begged me not to put more signs up and to quit asking questions. She feared for my life. My grandmother prayed.

My questions persisted. I asked my family and friends again if they knew anything at all. Perhaps the tight lips were afraid for me to learn hurtful things about my son. I tried facing the truth about Jabbo's involvement. Maybe if I acknowledged his criminal activity, then surely folks would open up and I could get the answers I needed.

Still, the answers did not come, and I was tormented by my imagination and more questions. Weirdly, my torment led me to wonder about random things too. For example, why did Jeremy not have on his jewelry? He loved his jewelry and always wore it. I asked Ruby about the jewelry. At first she denied knowing anything, but two or three days later, she called to say she had found his jewelry on top of their refrigerator in their apartment. This made no sense and probably was totally unconnected. My suspicions mounted.

Finally, after maybe six months, I called the police and asked, "Is there anything to report?" Sensing their impatience with me, I cried out, "Please, why won't you help me? Why won't you help?" I hung the phone up and collapsed in my frustration. Lord, I screamed out to you, "Why, God? Why?"

A few days later, the young woman detective who had worked the case the first few days and had been sympathetic called me at work. She asked me to come down to the station as soon as possible. I immediately stopped my work and left to meet her. My hopes were lifted as I thought, Finally, there is news. I prayed all the way that I would be strong, and I thanked you,

God, because justice was going to be served at last. I would have my answers and confront the reality of Jeremy's murder.

When we got to the station, the young detective was there to greet me. She didn't look jubilant or as thrilled as one should be after solving a murder. In fact, she broke down and cried. She told me the eyewitnesses to the murder could not identify any of the perpetrators because it was too dark to see their faces. Finally, shaking her head, she mustered up enough courage and said, "There is nothing more I can do on this case. We don't have enough evidence for an indictment. I'm so sorry."

Stunned, Mr. Panama and I walked out of the station, got in my car, and drove back to work. My ears were ringing with her words, my voice defiled the silence around me, and I screamed at the top of my lungs. My soul wailed in despair.

For my soul is full of troubles, and my life draws near to the grave.

Psalm 88:3

The Guilt

O God, the shock threw me into a place I had never known. After months of trying to reconstruct my son's murder, suddenly I was told all the pieces to the puzzle had been thrown into the air and where they landed made no difference. It mattered not that some of the pieces were upside down, turned sideways, or had torn and bent edges. The puzzle was unsolvable. It wasn't supposed to happen this way. Life was not like this on television, where murders are always solved and justice prevails. I had worked endlessly to make sense of things, and now I was told there was "insufficient evidence." My questions had all been in vain, and I was completely powerless. The sinking feeling in the pit of my stomach moved up to my heart, filling it with a cold hollowness. The void made me puke.

His words "Nothing will ever make you happy" flooded my thoughts again. I exited the door of shock and opened another to stare face-to-face with a room filled with guilt-my guilt. Entering with trepidation, I realized this is where I belonged. After all, parents are supposed to protect their children, no matter the cost. I had failed this responsibility miserably. Along with my failure, I had altered the progression of nature and the natural order of life. Even the special calendared events of holidays and birthdays were now changed forever from excited anticipation to dread. All the days of my life were the same. From the time I got out of bed until I laid my head on the pillow of sleeplessness, each day was filled with loss, and I was to blame.

My guilt required punishment. Reviewing my guilt over and over was part of my punishment for altering nature's design. Strangely, this self-deprecating exam was beneficial in my need to keep Jeremy with me forever. In my guilt, I rationalized that since I didn't pay enough attention to my son in life, I would be forever available to him in death. I would not walk away from this pit of despair because it was a fair and just punishment for my failure.

God, I think guilt is something you bear alone. My guilt fluctuated from early acts of naughty peevishness in my childhood to the sexual desires of adolescence to my adult years of worshiping materialism. Guilt stacks up, layer by layer, until a mountain looms over you.

The guilt of my youth had been neatly folded away in the attic of my mind for years and years. Now I unpacked it, held it up for examination, and determined I would wear it every day. I remembered all the times I had let my dad down. I failed him by not living the righteous life he had always preached about from the pulpit. I walked in sin, resenting people in our church who shunned my mother and me. I experimented with sex in my early teens instead of honoring my body as God's temple. Getting pregnant before marriage and being so young broke my father's heart and killed his hopes and dreams for me. Lusting after one man then another created more grief for my dad and the entire family. Typically, I might feel sorry at first for failing my dad, but my selfish desires quickly put me back on the wrong path. Somehow failing my father foreshadowed my failures as a mother. The sins of my youth built a good foundation for the mountain of guilt that was growing

As a young mother, I admit it was easier to let my mother, dad, and grandmother provide care for Jeremy. It was easier to follow an exhausting schedule of school, work, church, and friends than to be tied down to a crying baby twenty-four hours a day. I martyred myself by telling everyone that I was sacrificing for my baby to have a better life. Of course, I wanted the best for my baby, but the truth is I was scared to be a mother. I was still a child myself, and maybe I was jealous of the time and attention Jeremy demanded. I had dreams and desires that needed to be realized. Parents were supposed to put the needs of their children ahead of themselves. Instead, I had settled into a routine of going ahead with my life and leaving Jeremy's needs to be met by others. O God, how can my baby ever forgive me?

I loved my boy, and he loved me back. I'm sure I was responsible for Jeremy's shortcomings. He was definitely a people pleaser, and whether he inherited this trait or adopted it from my example, I never knew. I remembered how unhappy he was with my decision not to let him go to New York. I insisted he stay and go to college; he complied in order to appease me. He only wanted to make me happy—the same thing I did with my own father. Jeremy was smart and business savvy. I proudly claimed these gifts of intelligence from my gene pool. I was busy working with two jobs and going to school to get ahead, but I failed miserably at steering him toward a legitimate career. In fact, I closed my eyes to many of the warning signs as his choices began to emerge. First, he ran with the wrong crowd. Secondly, he dropped out of college. Then there were calls from the police asking me if I knew about cash found in his car. But the most important sign was how our relationship suffered from angry, hurtful fights and periods of stubborn silence. I often confronted him about the thugs surrounding him, about the police calls, and about going back to school. I would preach about the ills of fast cash, telling him he had to work hard to achieve his goals.

It wore me down being the "bad guy." Frustrated, I grew tired of the confrontations. God, forgive me for my ineffectual attempts at parenting. They weren't good enough to combat the evils that swallowed up my son. I should have declared spiritual warfare. Instead, I grew weary, and in my weariness, I often closed my eyes to Jeremy's rapid decline. Refusing to open my eyes led him straight to his grave.

My guilt encompassed blaming a host of others for failing to help me save my son. Sometimes, God, burdened by my guilt, I found relief by using scapegoats to share the load. Unfairly, I blamed my pastor for not doing more to help my son. I asked him to speak to Jeremy about the people he was involved with, and he did, but it was useless. The truth was evident. I had waited too late to ask for help because I didn't want anyone to know what was happening to my son. I was ashamed of the things he was doing. People would blame me and say, "She sings the gospel, but she can't save her own son." It's funny how our thoughts become reality because I heard these very words the night Jabbo was murdered. Instead of exposing the full extent of my son's deep involvement in the drug business, I kept the ugly truth secreted away for two reasons. First, full exposure meant I would have to believe horrible things about my son, and no one wants to think the worst of their own child. I believed my hopes and dreams were closely connected with the successes of my child. By acknowledging the evil in Jabbo's life, I would have to admit my own failures. Secondly, and this was even worse than admitting my failures as a parent, I was worried about what other people would think when the secret was fully exposed. God, forgive me. It was easier to blame my pastor than to stand in the light of truth.

The blame game blew in another uglier direction. I remembered my brother and his cavalier efforts to keep Jeremy from going into the drug business. After drug dealers approached my brother about Jeremy's desire to work with them, I wondered why my brother had not come to me immediately with this information. How could my brother think it was better to be his money handler? Was that to protect my son? No, not in million years. That was incredulous. Whether my brother was already connected or saw a way to invest in the drug business, I was not sure what his interest was in this life of crime. In my mind, he was only interested in satisfying his own greed.

Beyond my brother's deceit, I learned my sister was twisted around my son's drug trade. She was addicted to drugs and alcohol, and this made it hard for me to understand. Naturally, in my eyes, she was in debt to feed her habit; however, I found out years later that she was working for Jeremy too. She confessed to me her involvement with a new illegal substance called "wet," made from embalming fluid. She was helping Jabbo test the market with this new product. Who does that? How could I not see what was going on in my own family?

Recently, a friend of mine did research and discovered that tobacco or marijuana cigarettes are dipped in embalming fluid, which is legally sold, and then laced with PCP or other illegal drugs. PCP, phencyclidine, is a strong hallucinogen that causes unpredictable psychotic episodes and violent behavior, giving it the reputation of a drug that causes users to act crazy. Only a tiny amount of PCP is needed to get high, but it can't be placed directly on the cigarette, so it is mixed with the embalming fluid first. The mixture is called "wet" or "water" on the streets. A dipped cigarette is called a "fry stick," and it sells for about twenty dollars. The high lasts from six hours to three days. The effects include visual and auditory distaste for meat. Other side effects may include coma, seizures, renal failure, and stroke.

O Lord, can you imagine how I felt after reading that my sister and brother were involved with my son in unleashing such utter destruction in our village? I felt betrayed by my family because I really did not know what "wet" was. For years I volleyed back and forth between denial and blame. On one side of the court, there was no way my sister and brother would ever be a part of this drug trafficking. After all, they were family. They loved Jabbo and me. Wouldn't they want to shield him as much as I did? On the flip side, why didn't they respect or love me enough as a single mother for trying to raise a son and provide for him? Wouldn't my brother and sister love their nephew enough to keep him from harm? Denying their involvement and blaming them more than troubled me for years. This debate burned and branded deep within my heart, and I have scars that have not yet faded.

I hung some of Jeremy's friends from the tree of blame too. How could true friends blindly follow someone down the wrong path? There is only one answer, and that is greed. Many of these boys grew up with Jeremy, played ball with him, and even sat together with him in church. They sat down at my table and shared meals with us. I loved all his friends, and I thought they cared for me or at least respected me. Not only did they have no respect for me, but they had no regard for the law. They relished the lifestyle Jeremy's drug business provided for them. Supposedly, several of these guys acted in roles as bodyguards; they failed. One of his newer friends, an older man who tended the bar my son frequented before his murder, actually approached and informed me he thought the world of Jeremy. In fact, he thought of him as a son. Well, what kind of a "fatherly friend" allows drug dealing in and around his business establishment? This man was aware of and most likely participated in the drug trade at that bar.

I wondered if Jeremy ever realized his friends betrayed him. O Lord, I tried to warn him over and over about the people he chose to call friends. For years after the murder, I was wary about anyone who claimed to be my friend.

My blame spilled over into the neighborhood. How could they not reach out and help identify my son's murderers? Didn't Jeremy always try to help the neighbors? He never wanted anyone to go without food or shelter. He often made provisions for them. Why didn't someone step up and identify my son's executioners? How quickly they forgot the good Jeremy did for the neighborhood.

Surely it was human nature for me to blame the police department. Sometimes I would blame them for being connected with the drug cartel. At times I accused them of looking the other way while a dealer was disposed of and taken off the streets. Other times I blamed their insensitivity, thinking "black-on-black" crime. O God, blaming others was my only consolation. There was no other explanation. Someone had to be blamed.

In my guilt, the final spew of shocking reality erupted, spraying pellets of hurt, anger, and shame. They stacked up like mortar and bricks, forming high walls of hardened bitterness. The walls loomed over me and around me, locking me into a chamber of torture. Escape was impossible, no way to get around or over such barriers. I rationalized my only choice was to hit the walls head-on. If I went too slowly, I would hit the wall and stumble backward, only to be stunned and forced to stand again and face the walls over and over. If I ran at it full throttle and hit the walls with all my resolve, I might get lucky and crash hard enough and not survive. I chose to run at it full throttle, hoping to die and break free from the torture chamber. I was consumed with rage, a broken heart, and shame. This was like being buried alive in a horror movie.

I knew Jeremy as my baby, a toddler, and an active little boy who loved me. I remembered him running through the neighborhood, fetching all his friends to come to church. I remembered trying to protect him from falls, fever, and scrapes. I remembered his smile as I put bandages on his boo-boos. I even remembered how proud I was to watch him shoot baskets. When he walked across that stage during graduation, I thought my heart would pop out of my chest. I loved him because he wanted to see his mama happy; he wanted to hear me sing. He often reminded me of myself a little. He wanted to please everyone, and he had a tender heart. He couldn't bear for anyone to hurt, and he believed there was a higher calling to make a difference in the world. I adored this son.

I did not recognize the young man who was executed in the alley because of a drug war. I did not know or I refused to recognize the man my son had become. O Lord, this was too much, too much. I could not bear this burden. I no longer knew who Jeremy Johnson was, and I thought I knew him. I thought we had a good mother-son relationship. I was either wrong or blinded, and I denied the truth. My son became someone I never wanted him to be. Never in my wildest imagination did I ever think it was possible for my son to live and die in the world of drugs and destruction. God, please forgive my child for his sins.

My son was caught up in evil. He was a drug dealer in South Dallas, and he distributed drugs to runners who sold to junkies. I prayed he did not sell to children and lure them into a life of addiction. He saw dealing as a fast way to make a lot of money to pay for the dreams he had as a boy. I heard from some of his friends, those in the business with him, that he was looking to make that final big deal and then get out of the drug business.

Whether this was true or not, I would never know. Did the "higher-ups" get wind of his desire to leave? Was this the reason why he was executed? No matter what I questioned or rationalized, my son chose his own path. It was not what I ever wanted or intended, but he alone was responsible for choosing the life of a drug dealer. He was taught right from wrong and was raised in the church. He professed his faith and declared his love for you, O Lord, yet he steered his life away from you in a very wrong direction.

No mother wants to learn her child chose evil over goodness. In my heart, I never believed this was possible. I had blamed myself, the neighborhood, and his friends who led him astray, and even you, God. How could you, a loving God, allow a precious child to choose a life of crime and corruption? This was inconceivable. Hadn't I prayed for you to step in and change Jeremy's life? I prayed constantly for you to help. I needed you to be a magician and make my son into the man I wanted him to be. I wanted a miracle.

For many years I continued to hit wall after wall in my chamber of guilt. I would knock down one wall of anger, only to find another block of shame. I would kick at a wall of gut-wrenching hurt, only to be stunned, facing another. I wanted to take the blame for my son and cover his sins. I hated to face the wall of my son's own guilt. Was there no other way? If I could have died for my son, giving him one more chance to turn his life around, I would have gladly laid down my life. Forgive me of my sin and for not being a better mother. Help me to forgive those I blamed. Again, I beg you; forgive my son for falling from your grace.

O Lord, my trials and tribulations were more than I could bear. Life was not worth living.

Have mercy on me, O Lord, for I am weak; O Lord, heal me, for my bones are troubled. My soul also is troubled; But you, O Lord how long? Return, O Lord, deliver me! Oh save me for Your mercies' sake! For in death there is no remembrance of You; In the grave who will give you thanks? I am weary with my groaning; all night I make my bed swim, I drench my couch with tears. My eyes waste away because of grief, it grows old because of all my enemies. Depart from me, all you workers of iniquity; for the Lord has heard the voice of my weeping.

Psalm 6:2-8

PART 5
Darkness before Dawn

Isolation was my companion for fifteen years after the murder of Jeremy. Mostly I thought of isolation in terms of detachment. My isolation was self-imposed. I detached from the world. The word detachment sounded harsh, abrasive, but to me it harmonized beautifully with the pain.

As Bishop Jeffery Thomas Sr. preached:

God did not intend for man to be isolated from one another. God created man in his own image to tend the garden of Eden. God, the creator, you declared in Genesis 2:18, "And the Lord God said, it is not good that man should be alone; I will make him a helper comparable to him." So you, O God, created a helper-or, a better term, helpmate-for Adam to govern the garden under your holy sovereignty. You desired man to be contented in relationship with each other in the garden. After eating the forbidden fruit, Adam and Eve were banished from the garden to live in a world full of thorns and thistles. Though banished, they were not separated or detached from one another. Sending mankind out into the world, arm in arm, was a generous provision for our survival, not just to increase our species, but to bless us immeasurably with family and friends.

My detachment began long before Panama Jack sailed from my life. I was on the lookout for the island of exile shortly after realizing I was not going to be allowed to die. I figured the next best thing was to be left alone with my sufferings. This meant detaching from the docks of despair and setting my sail for a safe place void of human relationships. After all, relationships with family, friends, or lovers were havens for misery. Everyone was banking on me to be strong, "get over it," and manage my life so I could sing praises again, lifting their spirits high. I was looking for obscurity, a place where no one would recognize me or my pain. I needed a shelter with opaque windows to prevent anyone from seeing me or my suffering. There was no need for light to shine and expose my tears. The darkness was preferable. Yes, only the cover of darkness would make my island of exile a safe hiding place for years and years. I doubted there would be comfort, but I hoped that hiding my tears might keep the scars hidden from others, as well as from me.

The old adage "The darkest hour comes just before the dawn" never occurred to me. I thought once I discovered my private island, I could manage the daily grind of living until the dark snuffed out my light.

Nightmare

Each morning I dragged out of bed or off the couch with the television still flickering from being left on all night. It helped to keep my mind turned off in case I actually drifted into a trance. I prayed for partial nights of comas and unconsciousness. I dreaded nights of RRTs (rapid, repetitive thoughts) and UTTS (uncontrolled tossing and turning).

After showering, dressing, and usually no breakfast, I set off for work. I tried going back to work two weeks after Jeremy's murder, but I struggled to get through each day. During the early post-murder weeks, still being in my shock mode, I paid little attention to what I was doing or what was being said. I'm sure words of kindness and sympathy were expressed by coworkers, and hopefully I acknowledged everyone with a nod or lowering of my head. As the days and weeks passed, I sensed awkwardness every time I entered the store. Having a new supervisor made me feel even more uneasy.

I was at work one day, sitting at my desk, and a weird thing happened. I thought it was a stroke. My vision was blurred, my ears rang a deafening silence, and my body seemed paralyzed. I sat for an eternity, hoping no one would walk by and notice me. Somehow I managed to reach for the phone and dialed my doctor's office. I babbled over the phone to the nurse, and she kept me on hold while she talked with the doctor. He wanted me to come to his office immediately. Panicking but trying to look calm, I managed to get my purse and told my coworkers I was going to lunch. I walked out, willing my body to move forward to get out of that place.

I was waiting in the examination room, scared I was having a stroke. I could hardly breathe, and I was sure my blood pressure was sky-high. When the doctor walked in, he looked at me and said, "What's happening, Rikki?"

That's when the dam broke. My tears washed over me like huge rollers in rough seas. I shook and writhed in pain; I grabbed my chest. Maybe this wasn't a stroke; maybe it was a heart attack. I reached for the doctor to help me, to give me medicine, to stop the aching. Instead of calling for the nurse or reaching for the defibrillator, the doctor stretched his arms open to me, and I buried my head into his chest, sobbing tears of pent-up grief. Oddly, I felt disconnected to my body having this strange attack. It was eerie, but I thought I was in the middle of an out-of-body experience, witnessing myself crying in the arms of the doctor.

My crying lasted nearly an hour. When the doctor pulled me away from him, he sat me down gently in a chair and sat down next to me, holding my hands. He compassionately informed me I was depressed and having an emotional breakdown. He thought I should be hospitalized, but I refused, because I could not bear for my family or others to know my situation. I wanted no one to snoop and explore my island of exile.

The doctor consented to no hospitalization as long as I agreed to start antidepressants and see a psychologist. He faxed over a doctor's order to my employer recommending a medical leave of absence. I went straight home and told no one what had happened or that I had taken a leave of absence.

I picked up my prescription and stared at the pills for a long time. I wondered if they would make me feel better, numb me, or just sedate me. I thought about taking an overdose. It crossed my mind that if I died, I might be able to see my baby again. Maybe he would meet me at heaven's gate. I called and made an appointment for counseling sessions.

Not knowing what to expect from a psychologist, and not knowing what was required of me, the sessions became increasingly difficult and tiring. I thought the whole purpose in going was to feel better. Instead, I got annoyed. She provoked me with questions about trust issues or about my state of mind at 2:00 p.m. in November 1992. The questions were random. I would respond with something to fill the silence, and she would check her watch to see if our hour was finished. Repeatedly, she would compare my situation to the bombing of the Murrah Federal Building in Oklahoma City. Perhaps my brain was clouded, but in my opinion, the sessions were ridiculous. The counseling ended after the third session.

Lord, I did not turn to you. In my guilt and anger, I was both ashamed of my depression and hurt that you didn't magically take away my trials and tribulations. Instead, I turned my life over to Mr. Panama. He took care of everything-all my bills and living expenses-and he helped me take care of my mother and grandmother. With Mr. Panama's help, I managed to hide from the world for about seven years.

My physical health took a toll too. I lost too much weight, had trouble eating, and my sleep patterns were strange. Often I laid down during the day in the hopes of blocking out my thoughts. At night, either I fell in the bed and drifted off, only to awaken an hour later, wrestling through the rest of the night, or I simply never closed my eyes. The RRTs drove me crazy. My racing heart thumped out of my chest. I hated the days because I might run into someone I knew and have to make small talk, but the nights were true nightmares! I dreaded and feared the nights. My anxiety started building every day around 4:00 p.m. knowing the night was quickly approaching

I was not able to work that first year. Besides the overwhelming sadness, my depression took on more anger and mistrust. I had lost all confidence with the police, thinking they had botched the investigation. I might never know who killed my child. The neighborhood turned their backs on me when I asked for help in finding my son's killers. Never again would I ask for anything from anyone. Feeling betrayed by my brother and sister, I trusted no one. My faith was put to the test, to say the least. God, our Father, my frustration turned angry and bitter. Not only had there been no miracle to change my situation, but things worsened. My prayers stopped.

Life was a farce. At home, I found safety in my detachment. Out in the world, I put on a façade. I was the strong, loving daughter and granddaughter who cared for my loved ones. Whether it was shopping, doctor appointments, or anything else needed by Mommy or Gee-Gee, I was there with a hug and a smile. As their health declined, I helped to provide for their care. Everyone thought I was a wonderful, loving daughter and granddaughter. Lord, I did love them, and I wanted to do the best for them, but my soul was saturated with pain that caused me to fall short.

In between 2001 and 2006, I lost Gee-Gee and then my mother. I went through the motions of burying them and missing them, but somehow my grief was not nearly as unbearable as I had imagined. Maybe that was the difference in natural causes of death compared to murder. Sometimes I would cry for my mommy and end up hysterical thinking about my son. If I found myself missing my mother and grandmother and those thoughts slipped ahead of the grief for my son, I easily pushed away these feelings to make room for Jeremy. I was caught between remaining loyal to my son and missing my sweet mommy and Gee-Gee.

The rolling tides of my life continued. Each morning I got out of bed, dressed, and drove to work. Being at work filled my time, and sometimes "busy work" filled my thoughts. I caught myself pouring over numbers on an expense report and realized my mind had separated from the suffering for a brief moment. Those times were like admiration for a garden after weeding and watering. I called these "oasis moments" because they were so few and far between. After work, I came home and roamed the house, looking for something to divert me until bedtime. I seldom missed choir practice on Wednesday evenings or Sundays at church. My singing continued in church because I was expected to sing. Many people thought I was a strong Christian, believing I had placed my faith in God's hands. I sang praises to you, O Lord, but I seldom noticed the words. The praises were sung for everyone but me.

Ironically, Pastor C. C. McNealy asked me nearly every Sunday to sing "Peace Be Still." In his compassion, he thought the message would reach me, inspire me, and deliver me. I sang the words beautifully and inspired the congregation, but the words were lost to me. Some people noted my devotion, but Pastor McNealy recognized my sorrow and continued asking me to sing this very song for almost one year. Perhaps he knew it was going to take some time before I could hear the words to this amazing song. At the time, I hadn't realized you, my Savior, neatly stored away the words, tucked them safely in my heart to use as salve in healing me for the many years ahead.

The winds and the waves shall obey thy will,
Peace be still.
They shall sweetly obey thy will.
Peace, Peace be still.
Hints of Dawn

I spent lots of time in bed thinking about all my sin and aggressions. Convinced that my sins caused Jeremy's death, I plotted ways for atonement. In my heart I wanted forgiveness, but I knew in my head that nothing would bring my baby back to life. I continued going to church, for some strange reason. Either it was such a habit or subconsciously I was hoping I could make amends by attending church and singing. My Sunday routine drained me of energy. My body performed with smiles and songs, but the taxing charade played havoc with my soul.

After not working that first year, a friend opened a new business and asked me to help her in the new venture. I was able to work, but I didn't consider the job as anything more than a means of making money and a way to help pass the endless hours. After another year, I left that job and began working at a clinic for the next ten years.

Again, my body performed all the necessary tasks required of my job, but my spirit was tired of life.

Mr. Panama was gone from my life for good, and I truly was alone for the first time in my life. I had been on the island of exile for years, so there was no need to adjust to being single again. No single person on earth knew my despair. It was hidden deeper than a black hole in the farthest depths of space. The grief was my own and mine alone.

After the death of my godfather, Pastor C. C. McNealy, it was not easy to stay in my church. There were too many painful memories and secrets hidden in the halls of the church. Friends and family members convinced me to come and start a new church with them. It was complicated to be disconnected yet remain close to those who considered me a friend. I did not want to let anyone down again. Grief did not take any particular shape. There were no rules, no boundaries to show me how to evolve in my mourning or how to continue with human relationships. So together, in 2006, several of us started the Koinonia Missionary Baptist Church. I attended, my voice sang sweet praises, and my grief silently clung to my heart. Holding on to the pain was my one sure way of never letting go of my child.

Along with no boundaries or rules for grieving, time also was not well defined. I had trouble remembering the days, months, and years. I was acutely aware of how each minute, each hour, and each day seemed endless. My time was void of new memories because I could not focus.

However, after about four years at my new church, a strange happening occurred, and it got my attention. I was singing a song I knew very well, but the words and the melody did not come out. I felt tears welling up in my eyes; I choked back emotions and started again. My sister tried to whisper the words to cue me, but nothing happened. Tears began to run down my cheeks. I ran out of church, crying silently, "God, what is happening? Aren't I trying to make amends for my sins for being a bad mother?" I was working, staying on the antidepressants, attending church, and singing. Sobbing, I asked, "What else am I to do, God? What do you want from me?"

This particular event in time was forever etched in my memory. Lord, I believed it was the first calling I dared to receive from you.

Certainly, my initial response was denial. It really didn't happen, did it? I was just in a blue mood and accidently let it slip out. There were no words falling from heaven, "Rikki, come follow me," like Jesus had said to Simon and the disciples. Besides, I was not in the right place with my life. I was still angry with you, O Lord, grieving my beloved son. My life was finished. I was filled with bitterness, anger, and sadness, not love and joy. I convinced myself there was no way you, O God, could use me. Not only did I feel unworthy of such a task-it was incredulous that you wanted me. In fact, I felt abandoned.

That same night after the incident at church, I had an eerie dream. I awoke preaching to thousands of people. I was proclaiming, "Live in Christ." Confused and scared, I went to my pastor. I reminded him of my leaving church in tears the previous Sunday, and then I relayed my dream. I asked him if there was a connection between the two. Did he think it was possible that you, God, were telling me to preach? He thought I misinterpreted the dream. Although he did not say it, I felt he was not convinced of my true desire to find out if you, God, were calling me. I went to him seeking answers. Instead, he found my questions intriguing. He suggested announcing to the church that I had a vision or perhaps I should consult with a female minister he knew. After this meeting, I was not comfortable discussing anything with him. I went back to my initial response of denial. No, God, you were not calling me to preach.

Tied to the church trauma and dream, another moment in time lingered around my memory track. This was a rare decision I made after Mr. Panama sailed to smoother waters. He made most of the decisions for the seven years we were together. The normal constants in my life before the murder were work, church, and family, and these remained the same after the murder on my island of exile. The decision started with a sense of responsibility for my family and friends who attended church with me. We had left our old church and started a new one. My grandmother always told me, "You made your bed, now sleep in it," but it simply felt wrong to sleep in this new church. I couldn't explain it to myself or to my family and friends why I had to move, but the new church was not where I belonged. Others had trusted my judgment, which was a huge mistake, considering the plaque of bitterness embedded in the walls of my heart. I tried to live up to their expectations for worship, even led them in several church matters, but I was confident that I had to move on.

My search led me to many different churches, though I had no intentions of joining any because I was not nearly ready to make a commitment. One of my visits took me to Mount Rose Church in Dallas. The bishop's words were so powerful that I continued visiting. Even though I was not in comfortable surroundings, it was the first time I was without family and friends. I didn't know what to expect, and I knew no one. I was a stranger, which could be good. I reasoned it would be easier to be unnoticed in this church since no one knew me or what had happened. I could easily remain anonymous and detached, or so I thought. On the one hand, I felt you, God, had led me to Mount Rose. On the other hand, I wouldn't allow you to take me out of my sanctuary of pain. I joined Mount Rose Church, where I was safe clutching onto my loss.

Stubbornly, I did not recognize these defining moments as hints of dawn coming. I was conflicted because I had accepted my fate of pain, yet there seemed to be a desire to acknowledge God in my life. Living in isolation kept me spiritually dry even though I attended church regularly. Thankfully, the church had been a constant in my life for as long as I could remember. I had known joy as a little girl in my father's church. He had preached about the church being a hospital for healing sick souls. Was it possible to know joy even in the midst of suffering? Lord, little did I know that the church would help release me from the bondage of anguish and despair. Even so, I remained hidden in church.

And I also say to you that you are Peter and on this rock I will build my My church, and the gates of Hades shall not prevail against it. And I will give you the keys of the kingdom of heaven, and whatever you bind on earth will be bound in heaven, and whatever you loose on earth will be loosed in heaven.

Matthew 16:18-19

PART 6
Reap for Joy

After fifteen years of carrying murder in my heart, I was growing weary. For most of those years, I contemplated killing myself, but I didn't want to hurt my family. I exiled myself on an island and detached from the real world. I lived in grief because I feared letting go of my son, and I allowed my guilt to imprison me for far too long.

That's when the word live came to me loud and clear from the CD I listened to at work. I struggled with living again, and I was scared. Living meant opening my heart up to more pain and heartache. Lord, I was not ready to join the world of the living again. You were persistent, and you kept live in my head until I began to grasp in my heart that you had a plan for my life. To live meant I would have to move away from the island of exile where I hid for fifteen years. I would have to let go of my son's murder, and I would have to focus on more than my sufferings.

Still, I was not willing to give up grieving. Life without my son was pure misery, and nothing would ever change what happened. I deserved to suffer, didn't I? Nothing could help me erase all that had happened and continue on with life while my son was buried in the ground. It simply was not the way nature intended.

Oddly, the hard-shelled armor of denial must have fractured for a brief moment because my random thoughts were frequented with old recollections of joy, interrupting the sadness of fifteen years. Most of these were thoughts of my family. I felt myself smiling as I scanned the pictures in my thoughts.

The first recollection was of my father calling me "special." As a little girl, he preached that "God is love." Though I often thought I had failed him, he urged me on to be the best I could be. When I was close to death, he called upon the elders in the church to pray with him for my healing. He exemplified a life lived responsibly based on his knowledge of the scriptures and through his faith in God. I respected my father, and he was a good man that made me feel special. I knew he loved me even when I continually disappointed him.

Secondly, my mother protected me from the wrath of mean-spirited people in our church. She taught me to love music. I used to plead with her during one of her tongue-lashings to me, "Mommy, stop talking so much." Somehow she always knew the right thing to do in any situation. She buried my baby girl and stood beside me to bury my son. Her compassion came from pain in her own life, and she soothed me with gentleness. Mommy was my protector, and I felt loved by her.

A third recollection popped into my thoughts about both of my grandmothers. I envisioned them with aprons on, hands on their hips, shaking a finger at me, all the while hiding smiles behind their dish towels. Both of them lived their lives trusting God, enduring hard times, and relishing all that's good. Humor flowed rather than bitterness. They prayed for me. Gee-Gee prayed me out of more than one bad situation. They were consistent in reprimands and sage sayings. I deliciously remembered cream cake and lemon pie made especially for all of the grandchildren. I admired them, and I knew they loved me.

The fourth was remembering my son's christening, Before the christening, my father spoke about the meaning of christening a child so we could easily understand. He said that christening was a sacrament where God the Father claimed Jeremy as his own. At the time, I did not ponder this profound truth. Thinking back on my own father laying hands on my son, saying, "Jeremy Jerrod Johnson, I christen you in the name of the Father, the Son, and the Holy Ghost," I wanted to remember that moment as sacred and holy. O God, you claimed my son because you loved him. He was yours to begin with, and maybe the time had come for me to hand him back over to your care. Thank you, O Lord, you picked Jeremy up and carried him in your loving arms, away from the evil of that cold night. You redeemed him as your child. He was safe forever in eternity with you.

Though the hints of dawn were realized and the recollections of loving relationships stirred up feelings of happier times, I still wondered if these were messages from you, O God. Was it time to let go and let you rebuild my life? What was your plan for me? I thought back over the story of my entire life. There were good parts, but certainly the sorrow of losing my son far overshadowed and consumed me for a big chunk of my life. There was a certain amount of control I sensed over my life of pain. I feared leaving this familiarity. I was skeptical of moving into the unknown, even if you were leading me forward. Could you turn my tears of sorrow into joy? Were you, O God, chiseling away at that crack in my armor? I offered you, my heavenly Father, my tears.

Those who sow in tears shall reap in joy. He who continually goes forth weeping, bearing seed for sowing, shall doubtless come again with rejoicing, bring his sheaves with him.

Psalm 126:5-6

The Beginning

The thought of speaking to a crowd of people was frightening, but singing was different. There were no anxious minutes preceding a concert in church. I was perfectly content to get up and belt out a song. Singing was similar to prayer time. I wasn't sure if you heard my prayers in the conventional way (kneeling, hands together in the form of a steeple, eyes closed, and head bowed), but deep down I was convinced you could hear my voice singing loud and clear. Singing in front of the church made no difference to me, because I tuned everyone else out except for you, O God, and me. At least this is what I wanted to believe. I figured it was one-sided because my voice was so loud and I didn't hear your voice. There was no obliging you, O Lord, with a listening ear. I was not a responsive audience to hear your music.

After joining my new church in 2010, I became aware of people during my singing. I saw faces glowing with smiles, hands lifted upward, and bodies swaying rhythmically. There was a new emotion welling up in me, and I felt a connection. I was singing alone, yet I could feel their voices singing with me. My voice was their voice, and together we were singing to You; however, this didn't happen when I sang at my home church. Probably my emotions just did not let me see or hear. I was delighted the first time I experienced this phenomenon. The second time it happened, I was awed, and the third time, I knew this was not a coincidence. Something was happening, and I suspected you, O God, were directing the choir of my life.

A thought came to me in the spring of 2010, and I relished in the idea that maybe this thought was the voice of the Holy Spirit. At this point, I had not looked back and begun to put the pieces of the puzzle together. I had not reflected on all the hints of dawn you were sending, but I was aware that interesting things were happening. Work was becoming a challenge, and it was no longer tedious and tiring. I found myself recharged after work, and I actually looked forward to Bible study on each Tuesday night. Above all, my passion for singing was soaring, and that passion gave rise to the thought of performing for all my friends and family. I wanted them to recognize something different about me. I wanted to thank my new friends at church who showered me with their acceptance. Was having a concert a fleeting thought? The more I thought about it, the more appealing the idea became. I felt giddy for the first time in forever.

I met with Reuben Mosley. After Jeremy's murder, Reuben continued checking on me from time to time. I always appreciated these kind gestures, although seeing him sometimes brought tears to my eyes, remembering my son's childhood. He played the drums at my old church, and I often saw him even if we didn't chat. On one occasion, Reuben asked, "How are you doing, Rikki?"

I answered politely, "I'm good. How about you?" I pushed past the automatic response and asked him if he remembered Jeremy's dream of helping me produce a recording. Reuben immediately lit up and said, "Absolutely! Let me help." We talked excitedly for a few minutes and then made arrangements to meet at another time to begin brainstorming. O Lord, was all of this possible? I was completely caught up in the moment with emotions I had not felt for so long.

After meeting with Reuben again, I asked him what he thought about a musical performance at church, a reintroduction to my music. Reuben jumped on the idea and added that it would be a great venue for announcing our intentions of recording my first CD. He thought maybe it would be a way to raise money to help with the expenses of recording, such as purchasing studio time. Reuben's excitement was contagious.

Our plans began to take shape. All the details easily fell into place. I believed that things went so smoothly, because Reuben insisted on praying over every detail. He made me laugh. I found myself praying to you too. O *Lord, please bear Reuben's prayers! Then I would quickly add, Thank you, Lord, for answering Reuben's prayers.*

I actually wanted to sing for all my friends both old and new. It would be my way to let everyone know I was alive again, since no one had any idea I had been dead for fifteen years. Living again took some getting used to, and I was working hard to stay plugged in. I found myself praying fervently throughout the day, not just at night. I prayed, Is this concert your will, God? Reuben was so positive and enthusiastic that it was getting easier to trust his vision for me. I wanted assurance that his vision was also yours, O God.

May 23, 2010, was the date of the concert at my old church. The morning before the concert, I was excited and nervous but still a little skeptical whether this was the right thing to do. Reuben was flying around all over the place, taking care of the last minute arrangements. He set up extra chairs, and I asked him why on earth he would do that. He rejoiced and said, "Rikki, the house is going to rock today, and we need to make room for all God's people!"

He checked out the sound system, set up a video camera, and moved furniture off the pulpit. I laughed and told Reuben he would make a great manager. I whispered a little prayer, "God, if nothing good ever happens again in my life, please know how joyful my heart is at this very moment. It feels good to live."

It was time. The plan was for Reuben to give a brief introduction, and I would walk down the aisle from the back of the church. I was in position, listening for my cue to begin singing and walking down toward the front. What happened next took me completely by surprise.

Reuben welcomed everyone to the pre-release concert of Just Gospel, saying that was the title for Rikki McNeil's first CD. He told them how special this concert was going to be and that it would be "life changing." I heard Reuben begin his introduction with a quick synopsis about my roots in gospel music taking me, with your help, all the way to a recording career. He was sharp and quick-witted, and he related so well with the audience. Then he paused in his speech, drew a deep breath, and said the only way he could introduce Rikki McNeil was by reading something he had prayed about and written. He shyly said, "It is a little bit poetry, a little bit music, and a whole lot of love for Rikki." He introduced me like I never could have imagined. Reuben shouted with joy, and you, God, painted a rainbow through my tears.

> Rikki sang that song
> You know that song you've been singing in
> your spirit,
> The one that helps you make it through the day?
> Rikki sang that number
> I woke up wondering how to start my day.
> Rikki sang, "Praise Him if the Lord's Been
> Good to You, You Ought to Praise Him."
> Rikki sang that number.
> She sang, "Oh, How I Love Jesus," and I was
> *reminded,*
> *I do love Him when I'm searching for fortune*
> and fame.
> Rikki sang, "Only What You Do for Christ
> Will Last."
> Rikki sang that number.
> When I was going through a difficult time,
> Rikki sang, "Peace Be Still." I said, "I'm gonna

fix this situation," but
Rikki sang, "Step Back and Let God Have
His Way."
I said, "What should I do 'cause the pain hurts
so bad?"
Rikki sang, "Encourage Yourself in the Lord."
Rikki sang that number
"Why does God want to waste his time on a filthy person like me?"
Rikki sang, "He Looked Beyond My Faults
and Saw My Needs."
I asked, "How do you find him?"
Rikki sang, "When I See Jesus" "I Go to
the Rock."
Rikki sang that number
Although Rikki sang me through the good
and bad times,
I found myself down and weary after another
of life's blows.
Rikki sang, "You Need a Heavenly Mind."
I began to question, "Where is God?"
Rikki sang, "He's on the Main Line." "Call Him
up and tell Him what you want."
I said, "I need God right now to show up
and show out."
Rikki sang, "You Can't Hurry God."
I said, "I've tried and God has given up on me,
so I'm gonna throw in the towel."
Rikki sang, "Don't give up. God Is 'So Good."
I said, "I know he is, but based on what my eyes
can see, it's over for me and
Rikki sang *"It's Not Over Until God Says*
It's Over!"

The crowd stood up, clapped, and roared my name, "Rikki, Rikki, Rikki!" I started walking down the aisle. My hands were trembling, and my heart was pounding. My voice was quivering as I began, but in all the excitement, it grew stronger and stronger. There was purpose in each of my steps, yet each footfall was like a floating feather. I was marching toward you, O God, singing with all my might. Your glory was powerful and present at that very moment. My voice shouted from your highest mountaintop, and my joy spilled over from your eternal well. I felt refreshed with abundant life. Down the aisle I walked, singing praises to you, my Lord!

Come by here, Dear Lord.
I've been praying for such a long time,
Praying for some peace of mind.

Stepping out of character, I stopped singing, put the microphone down at my side, and paced from one side to the other. Then I stopped, bowed my head, and asked you to lead me in words to touch those who needed healing. The room was completely still and quiet. People must have wondered what I was doing. They probably thought I had missed my cue or forgotten my music. I stood with my head bowed until you, O Lord, scooted me forward. With an ounce of courage, I cleared my throat and uttered, "God is good. Amen!"

Instead of singing the next scheduled song on the program, I began to testify about my journey through the valley of the shadow of death. I talked about the many years of drowning in the ocean of despair. For the first time in fifteen years, I spoke about my son's murder. I even shared my desire to die and my thoughts of ways to end my life until you, O God, reached out and said, "I have other plans for Rikki." I told them you had other plans for them to live an abundant life too. All anyone needed to do was move out of the driver's seat and let you, O God, do the steering for the rest of the way. I prayed, "God is good! Amen."

I wasn't sure what to do after interrupting the concert with my testimonial, so I began to clap my hands to the rhythm of "If It Had Not Been for the Lord On My Side." My heart overflowed with joy and thankfulness. I felt you were standing next to me, encouraging me, and saying, "Daughter, in you, I am well pleased." The sense of harmony in my life was as delicious as any cream cake or lemon pie I ever ate! I thanked you, Lord, for being on my side. I sang this final song with all my heart and lungs.

> If it had not been for the Lord on my side,
> Where would I be? Where would I be?
> If it had not been for the Lord on my side,
> Where would I be? Where would I be?
> He kept my enemies away.
> He let the sun shine through on a cloudy day.
> Oh, he wrapped me in the cradle of his arms,
> When he knew I'd been battered and torn.

After the concert, my feelings were all over the map. I felt courageous, strong, and empowered, but above all, I had the truest feelings of humility. I had been in your presence, O God, witnessing to your people. I had no speech training, no speech writers or editors. I only had your power flowing through every word. At this special moment in time, you had used me for your plan, and I was humbled by this honor.

Many people stayed after the concert to meet me and thank me. Some enjoyed my singing; others were moved by my testimony. One woman came to me in tears, telling me she had thought of killing herself the night before. Now, through my words, she heard you offering her a new resolve to live. I prayed that you would give her strength and courage to live anew.

There were no words to describe what that concert meant to me. Besides celebrating my plans to record, I had wanted to testify about your redeeming power. You, O God, brought me back to life. Amazingly, the celebration provided me the biggest affirmation of all, and it was directly given by your Holy Spirit. Just as Reuben had said in his introduction that this concert would be "life changing," so it was. As for me, I was forever changed. Not only was I going to record an album, but I wanted to live, proclaiming your power. I wanted the world to know that you, Almighty God, are a restorer. You can repair damaged, battered, and ruined lives. I was honored to be in your service.

Sowing Seeds

Lord, you continued to amaze me. Reuben's wheels were spinning in his mind again. He didn't tell me until after the fact, because he never wanted to worry me, but after the concert, Reuben was researching online for recording studios that were interested in signing new artists. He came across one studio called the Tate Music Group. They had an online questionnaire that Reuben quickly filled out and sent back; there was no response. Disappointed, Reuben continued praying and searching for someone who might be interested in a recording contract. Four weeks later, Reuben was on his way to work when his cell phone rang. It was Monique Headley from the Tate Music Group in Oklahoma. She said she received the questionnaire and wanted to know more about Rikki McNeil.

Reuben told Monique about me, about the prerelease concert, and how amazing it was for everyone. Monique asked, "Where can I hear her music?"

Reuben responded, "Nowhere! But I will send you a CD, DVD, and biographical sketch of Rikki."

"That's not really the way we do things, but I suppose we can take a look at what you've got. I suggest you get these to me as soon as possible. I'll be in touch if we decide to pursue this any further," Monique replied curtly. She was all business, according to Reuben.

After scurrying around, Reuben made a CD of me singing and a DVD with various people commenting on my life and my singing. They were not the greatest quality, but satisfied, Reuben sent them on to Monique. He never told me why he was making these recordings, he only said he thought they might come in handy someday.

Another month or so passed, and Reuben was disappointed because he had not heard anything. He continued to search for other ways to get me recorded. Time and time again, he would receive e-mails from various music companies thanking him, but they were not interested. Then an e-mail came from the Tate Music Group thanking him for inquiring about their studio, but they did not offer to record me. Another e-mail came from Tate, which suggested all kinds of changes to be made. Needless to say, Reuben was more than discouraged, and he began to wonder if he should give up and wait on another recording company. He thought maybe God had another way into the gospel music industry.

One night, weeks after Tate had sent the previous e-mail, Reuben was driving home from work, checking his phone messages. That's when the call came. He didn't recognize the caller, but it was a lady. She left a message that said, "We want to offer Rikki McNeil a recording contract. Please call us at your convenience."

Reuben hooped and hollered all the way home. He wanted to call and tell me, but he thought better of that idea and decided to wait until he had the contract in his hands. He was afraid I would have a panic attack or fall over dead! Little did I know that sugar plums danced in his head all night long. The following morning, Reuben called the lady back.

She asked, "Are you Rikki?"

Reuben laughed. "No!"

"Does Rikki know that we want to sign her?" the lady questioned Reuben hesitantly.

"Nope." Reuben chuckled back.

The lady, hearing the humor in Reuben's voice, asked, "Why are you keeping this from her?"

"Because I don't want Rikki to panic like I did waiting on you all to make a decision," he belted out, grinning from ear to ear.

A FedEx package came two days later. Reuben called me immediately and said he needed to meet with me. Not able to keep a poker face any longer, Reuben rushed over to my house with the contract in his hand. I fell to my knees with thanksgiving. We went to Oklahoma and signed the contract at the corporate office. My shouts of joy were heard in every direction.

We started recording Just Gospel on January 24, 2011. I never imagined anything could be so exciting, We had to make arrangements for musicians and backup singers. There were contracts to sign with them. Travel and hotel arrangements had to be made for everyone because most of them were coming from Dallas. I had known them for a long time and performed with them, so I wanted them to be part of the recording process. We had to get permission from the songwriters to record some of the songs on the album. Fortunately, Reuben took care of most of the details, after all, he truly was my promoter, my agent, and my dear friend. I remembered that we had made a deal, and you, O God, had notarized our contract. I shouted with joy!

I have never been so tired in all my life. We woke early each morning and worked long hours. The first day, I went back to the hotel, took a shower, and put on my pajamas. I ordered room service for dinner because I was too tired to go out. I talked on the phone to Reuben and a few friends from home. As I lay in the bed thanking you, O God, I could not keep my eyes open. I slept like a baby.

For he who has entered His rest has himself also ceased from his works as God did from His.

Hebrews 4:10

The next five days were spent in the studio. It was thrilling. The studio folks first recorded just the music with the instruments, then the backup singers, and finally my vocals. They combined each part, breaking down every significant note over and over again, and finally spliced all the best combinations. The process of recording is fascinating, and I loved every minute of it. The recording studio made me feel like a celebrity.

One afternoon, I was taken to have my publicity shots done. I laughed at being treated like a star, especially when the photographer worked at posing me and said, "Ms. McNeil, who did your makeup?" Amazingly, she complimented me on being "put together nicely with great accessorizing." I felt great because I had done all of it. The shots were made with all my own clothes and jewelry.

Talk about feeling special. I surely did. I was proud, but not in a prideful, back-patting way. I was awed to be on your team and honored to know you would be using my voice. My songs would shout with joy and help sow seeds in the abundant garden of love. The drive home to Dallas felt more like flying on angel wings. We floated all the way back with excitement, planning and talking about the future.

Watering and Nourishing

Returning home meant I had to go back to my normal routine. Of course, I had to pay the bills, so back to work I went. I had been at my job for about four years, but I felt so invigorated and enjoyed being back to work. I thought for sure my coworkers could tell I was walking on air. I was so grateful to have my job, and I thanked you, O God, every morning upon my arrival and again at the end of the day as I left for home.

Church was still regularly scheduled with choir and worship. My prayer life was booming, and I prayed blessings for anyone who crossed my path. I learned what it was to love again. Since I knew your love for me, I loved everyone I ran into or met for the first time. I looked at them with your eyes and knew they had potential because they were your creations. I yearned to know you more, and I prayed to be all that you wanted me to be. My soul was ablaze, and I never wanted it to burn out. I wanted to protect myself against the desire to be a charred ember. It was time for me to become better acquainted with the Holy Word. I joined a new minister's class at my church. At first I was timid, but in a short time, I was drinking in the Scriptures and quenching a thirst I hadn't known before.

I spoke often with my bishop because I relished the fact you found me, saved me, and brought me back to life. Bishop Jeffery Thomas, Sr., was delighted for me, and he encouraged me to continue growing in the Scriptures as a means of sharing my testimony with others. He shepherded me with prayers and words of wisdom. Oftentimes, before I could even share that I was struggling with a particular scripture, Bishop Thomas would offer solutions through his sermons or teaching. Other times, when my "old baggage" came out and tried to pack me away, he would coin clever words like KIT, which he defined as "Keep it moving!" It was a blessing to be under the bishop's guidance at Mount Rose, to learn and prepare myself for your work, Heavenly Father.

On the first Sunday in 2011, I announced that God had a calling for me. I told my church that I was going to preach and sing for the glory of God. Furthermore, I told the congregation how I wanted all mankind to know that anything is possible with you. As soon as I said it, my mouth went dry, and I could hardly speak another word. Like Moses, I thought about protesting to you that I was not a good enough speaker to lead your people out of bondage. Realizing that I was committed, I did not protest. Instead, I prayerfully asked you to please make my knees stop shaking and if you would be so kind to direct me to the nearest water fountain.

One week later, I began a class to learn how to minister to God's people. I desperately wanted to be worthy as one of your servants, so I continually prayed. I asked you to open my ears to listen for your instructions; I prayed to be obedient. I felt a deep responsibility not only to sow seeds but to nurture any seedlings that may take root. You, O God, saved me, replanted me, and nourished me with your unfailing grace. Thank you, Father God, for loving me back to life. You have blessed me.

> You blessed me, Lord.
> Oh, you blessed me, Lord.
> When I woke up early this morning,
> Clothed in my right mind,
> Just can't keep it to myself.
> You blessed me, Lord.
> You blessed me, Lord.
> Lord, Lord, Lord. You've been good to me.
> You've opened doors in my life I was unable
> to see.
> You blessed me once, you blessed me twice.
> You've been blessing me all of my life.
> I just can't keep it to myself. You blessed me, Lord.
> You blessed me, Lord.
> This is my story. This is my song.

I've been praising my Savior all day long.
You blessed me once, you blessed me twice.
You've been blessing me all of my life.
I just can't keep it to myself.
You blessed me, Lord.
You blessed me, Lord.
Over and over,
You blessed me over and over!"

PART 7

Discernment and Wisdom

As these words are written, it is nearing the end of 2011. This marks more than sixteen years since my beloved son was murdered. It also marks the most remarkable year of my life. I am new again, refreshed and thriving in your love. Extraordinary things have happened this year, and I have done things I did not think were possible. I am dreaming again, and I am living out these dreams.

The CD is close to being released, and I continue to sing in concerts and give my testimony whenever you deem it necessary. I went to Chicago with my church to perform and was well received. The performance went out on YouTube, and I was played on the radio stations in Chicago. The story of my life is close to being completed and edited for publication. I am participating on panels to promote positive changes in our urban neighborhoods, churches, and businesses that would encourage our young people to aspire toward righteous living and away from drugs.

My church friends and family continually pray for me and my ministry. I continue to work hard to be the servant you want me to be. I study hard and find strength through my prayers. I know I have to get this right because members of my own family may look to me in leading them to your green pastures.

Dear, dear Reuben continues to manage all the bookings, finances, and promotions. He is my number-one cheerleader, always greeting me with a smile and a word of encouragement. Mostly, he prays for me and every step we take in this venture. No matter how the CD is received or how far my ministry reaches, I am confident Reuben will stay the course, because he is under contract with the Lord-signed, sealed, and delivered! For Reuben, I am most thankful, and I will continue to pray, Please answer Reuben's prayers!

Along with all the excitement of being in my new life, I have learned a great deal about myself this past year. Some things are important for me to acknowledge; others have been discarded as "not necessary" by you, O God. Discovery and acceptance of my divine purpose has revealed many changes in my new life. There are some parts of me that are the same as before I stopped living. I always sang with my voice, but now I sing with my soul. I still work because I have a mortgage, car payment, and I love pretty clothes.

The positives in my life are evident. I want to sing and talk to anyone who will hear about your love and power to heal. Beyond my voice, I have become a disciplined prayer warrior. I find prayer helps me to focus on you, so I pray all through the day. You are my constant companion, and you get an earful regularly from me. But my true focus on you, my Heavenly Father, comes when I am still and quiet. That is when I listen with my heart. You are my precious shepherd, and I don't want to miss one word, one thought, or one task you may be giving me.

Bible studies at church have provided me with a new discipline to stay in the Holy Word; I read Scripture every day. I was not a great student, and I did not enjoy reading in school. Now I find myself devouring the Word as if it were my first time ever reading the Bible. I am convinced that Scripture is the best source for meeting you and getting personally acquainted. The Bible is your way of revealing yourself to me. It is my resource book for self-improvement/self-help. I go to Scripture to discover your plan for me. The Bible is my road map as I journey with you, my abiding companion along the shores of life.

For fifteen years, my life had come to a dead end. Now I am traveling forward, content to go whatever speed you determine. Sometimes I am propelled forward quickly. At other times I take side trips to rest, soak it all in, and give thanks. Once in a while, a side trip leads me to the land of discovery. Even on a side trip, I shout with joy!

Here, I can pull out all my dirty laundry, sort it, wash it, and hang it up in the clean air to dry. In the sorting, I have found a few answers to perplexing questions. In the land of discovery, I am working hard to resolve issues from the trials and tribulations chapter of my life. I pray for discernment and wisdom as I take this side trip. Discernment is required if I am to keep my focus to live in your glory.

The speech pleased the Lord, that Solomon had asked this thing. Then God said to him, "Because you have asked this thing, and have not asked long life for yourself, nor have asked the life of your enemies, but have asked for yourself understanding to discern justice, behold, I have done according to your words; see, I have given you a wise and understanding heart, so that there has not been anyone like you before you, nor shall any like you arise after you. And I have also given you what you have not asked: both riches and honor, so that there shall not be anyone like you among the kings all your days. So if you walk in My ways, to keep My statutes and My commandments, as your father David walked, then I will lengthen your days."

1 Kings 2:10-14

Discernment and Wisdom for the Journey

The journey through this remarkable side trip was interesting but scary at times. There were moments of exhilaration but also moments of quiet resignation. It was important to take this detour. There in the land of discovery, all along both sides of Main Street, were scads of garages. Some were very old garages with worn out signs dangling from rusted-out poles; others were fancy, high-tech garages with multiple bays and signs that flashed "Open 24 Hours." There were garages for bodywork, lube jobs, and tire alignments and wheel balancing-all the necessary check-ups for keeping my heart, soul, and mind in proper running condition. If I would be a good servant, a 50,000-mile checkup would be a good idea. With all systems in good, working order, I could better travel up the entrance ramp leading to glory. This was where I would wave my flares in the hopes of directing people caught in bad traffic. Confidently, I would direct them toward your beautifully engineered highway to heaven.

The first garage I pulled into took a look at my spiritual alignment. There were a few kinks that tended to cause my steering wheel to pull toward the wrong side. Your holy head mechanic informed me that forgiveness was the best alignment for the soul.

With your grace, I could forgive. The first on my list to forgive were my son's killers. This was a work in progress. I would make headway, and then I slipped backward sometimes. Mostly, I gave this project over to you, O Lord, because I trusted you for my complete overhaul. As forgiveness took hold, surely you granted me deep peace and assurance that I no longer need to be their judge and jury.

The police report was made available to me just recently. I chose not to open it but gave it to Reuben; I trusted him with this report. There were discrepancies between the report and what I learned on my own through detectives, family members, and residents of the neighborhood. The report described that three young men, black males, met with my son outside of the bar. One of them pulled out a gun, and my son turned and ran across the street to an alley, trying to escape the gunman. The other two ran and jumped into a car, driving away from the scene. The gunman chasing my son fired many shots, including the one that struck him from behind and exploded through the femoral artery. This was the cause of Jeremy's death.

The report also indicated that an indictment was brought against the shooter. He went to trial, but on the first day in court, the case was dismissed against him. There was no paperwork of information listed with the court documentation as to why the case was dismissed, but it only stated that it had been dismissed. Now I realized why the lady detective cried and apologized to me; she said there was not enough evidence to try the case in the courts.

Shortly after the murder, the other two men gave eyewitness accounts, accusing the shooter. They both admitted to being at the scene of the crime, but they declared they were not involved directly with setting up my son. They were questioned numerous times and gave similar accounts. They each blamed the other for being there but adamantly pointed the finger at the third man, who had the gun. Apparently right before the case went to trial, these two recanted their original statements, as well as the few neighborhood bystanders, with their corroborating statements. Conveniently, there was no evidence for a conviction.

Interestingly, the two men who were with the shooter are now in prison, convicted of other crimes. One was sentenced to life imprisonment for being a habitual criminal. The other was sentenced to thirty years for murder, along with an additional twenty years for another offense. The man who shot my son is not in prison. There is no information on record about this killer.

With your grace, O God, I can forgive the men responsible for my son's death. I do not know why they took my son's life. I have no way of ever understanding the lack of regard for human life. I do know that illegal drugs cause crimes against your precious children. I pray for each of these men's lives. I pray you will restore them to the creations you intended. I pray, God, you will give me the spiritual eyes to see each man as you see him. I pray each may find peace and the desire to lead a productive, godly life. With your grace, I can love these children and forgive their grievous act of killing. You have given me the Holy Spirit, and you have breathed new life into me that moves me to forgive them. Forgiveness is possible with your Holy Spirit.

Receive the Holy Spirit. If you forgive the sins of any, they are forgiven them; if you retain the sins of any, they are retained.

John 20:22-23

The holy head mechanic suggested that I might want to go across the street to the eternal body shop to smooth out the dents and scratches from the hailstones of bitterness and resentment. The faithful body shop operator assured me that he could definitely buff out the damage, but it would cost a lot more than I anticipated. He said I would need to buy an additional forgiveness polish applicator and release buffer. He said it was a great deal because this was a dual repair for both the mind and the soul. It was sort of two-for-the-price-of-one. I opted to pay the extra price.

For years I was not able to reconcile loving my brother and sister. I hated them for their part in my son's destruction. I told you, O

God, that I felt so betrayed by both of them. How does one go about forgiving an act of betrayal?

I remembered my folks reminding me over and over that I was the oldest and I needed to always look after my little brother and sister. I thought I did a good job of being a big sister. I loved them even when I felt like the third man out.

I thought there would never be an adequate answer for why they betrayed me. Again, illegal drugs played a huge part in this betrayal, yet they were the ones who chose drugs over family. My sister was addicted, and this prevented her from managing and making good choices. Her life was unhealthy, and she lived within the chains of chaos.

My brother got caught up in the lure of fast money, as did my son. He was aware of Jeremy's tampering with selling drugs. It made no difference if my brother was involved with the drug cartel and groomed my son or if my son was responsible for their partnership in crime; either way it was a tragedy. My son was dead, and my brother's life was in peril.

Smoothing out the dents from their betrayal came from realizing they were your creations too, Lord. Their flaws have caused me so much grief, but knowing they are your children and a part of my family compelled me to forgive them. I do not condone their involvement with drugs. I will not look the other way when I see them participating in such destruction, but I will always love them, even if it is from a distance. In forgiving them, the resentments and anger were forever buffed out. The love for my brother and sister polished my soul, and forgiveness freed me from resentment and bitterness.

Forgiving my brother and sister was more than a two-for-one deal. Along with love polishing and freedom from bitterness came a precious extra bonus. You, O God, gave me the gift of compassion and mercy. I wanted my brother and sister to know that your love seeks them out. Your love is merciful and compassionate.

And be kind to one another, tenderhearted, forgiving one another, even as God in Christ forgave you.

Ephesians 4:32

Pulling out of the body shop, I realized it would be a good idea to get the tires of my heart balanced if I was going to stay tuned up for your work. Balancing my heart was vital because it actually would keep all the working parts of my mind and soul in sync. I knew this garage would perform a "do or die" operation of repair; it required balancing and rotating the tires of my heart.

For far too many years, I have blamed myself. I blamed myself for not fulfilling my father's dreams for me. I blamed myself for not being lovable enough to keep committed relationships with any man. I blamed myself for not providing more for my mother and grandmothers. Most of all, I blamed myself for my son's wayward life that resulted in his death. Since I failed my son in life, I wanted to succeed in being a loving mother in his death.

The heavenly balancer and rotator told me I was incapable of making these major adjustments. He called in the Holy Spirit and asked me to receive the only guaranteed way to a balanced life. Guess what. The Holy Spirit offered me forgiveness through Jesus Christ.

It was interesting to note that the task I dreaded the most was really the least burdensome. Forgiveness is the gift your Holy Spirit poured out. God Almighty, in your mercy and infinite wisdom, you forgave me-a flawed daughter, a flawed wife, a flawed mother, a flawed woman. Your Son, Jesus Christ, laid down his life to cover over my sinful flaws and made me right before you. By spilling his blood on that cross, he washed away my sins and restored my heart, my soul, my mind, and my life. Your Son, the Son of Man, died to give me life. If you, O God, can forgive me, can I do any less? I accepted the gift of your Son's blood that was shed for me. Shout for joy! I am forgiven! I am alive in Christ!

But that you may know that the Son of Man has power on earth to forgive sins.

> Mark 2:10

The final garage was a detail shop. It was here that my soul, my mind, and my heart were washed, waxed, and refreshed. The power washer smoothly removed most of the remaining traces of anger and bitterness from the worst sandstorm of my life. These traces included the police department, the courts, and even the neighborhood. Forgiving these traces was not too difficult; I realized entities like these are full of both self-serving people as well as selfless servants interested in the welfare of others. Sometimes the selfless folks go unnoticed while the selfish get all the attention. Either way, I recognized there were many who were selfless and offered compassion to me. For them, I gave thanks. Others were harsh, negligent, and uncaring; for them, I offered forgiveness.

The detailer of life decided I needed to go through the power washer again. He believed there was one large trace of residue remaining. He said that it was deeply engrained in the hood of my heart. It was the seed of blame and guilt. The final detailing required forgiveness of my son. I told the detailer of life that there was nothing for me to forgive my son for. He asked me to pray and reexamine this last bit of residue.

Prayerfully, I discovered that this was a gray area, and it needed my attention. Just as madras colors bleed together, so do the colors of disappointment, hurt, and even anger. They ran together, grieving my heart.

I have an idea how grieved you were by the sins of mankind, O Lord. You must have hurt beyond human understanding. I was grieved by the choices my son made on this earth. I was not able to exchange my life for his, though I would gladly have if given the opportunity. His death was partially a result of his wrong choices. I knew in my heart that Jeremy had a good heart, but he too was flawed. It's funny how a parent loves a child anyway. I loved Jeremy with all my being. I always hoped his goodness would overcome the bad. If there had been more time, Jeremy might have found his way back to your righteous path, Lord. Because of his wrong choices, he missed the most important opportunity of all here on earth-he missed out on serving the Almighty.

I forgave my son for making a grievous mistake. I forgave Jeremy for altering the natural order by dying before me. I forgave him for all the birthdays I could have celebrated, for all the grandbabies I did not have, for all the missed pleasures of doting on his successes.

I forgave him for all the lost years of opportunities we should have shared. Knowing you spared my son through your forgiveness and eternal love, I found contentment living my life on this side of eternity, sustained by sweet memories. I held tightly to your promise that one day I will see my son again. Whenever you, O God, place precious Jeremy in my arms once again, I will shout with joy.

At last I was cleansed and polished. The overhaul had given me a sense of freedom, and I was rearing to step on the accelerator and speed up the ramp to your holy highway. Just as I started my engines, the inspector of mercy ran out to remind me that I needed fuel and water for the remainder of the journey. What was I thinking?

The inspector of mercy directed me to the self-service area. I asked him, "How can I repay you?"

He boldly answered, "No problem, the cost has already been paid for you."

I knelt down and reached up to start the pump. Out flowed the blood of Christ shed for me. I was speechless. Reverently, I turned around to see the inspector of mercy. He handed me a basket of broken pieces from the bread of life. He told me, "Take this for the trip; you will need this for abundant life."

In awe and wonder, I started up my soul, my mind, and my heart. I turned to thank the holy inspector of mercy, but he waved me on, saying, "Go with God."

PART 8

The Mission

God is my Savior and my Redeemer. I have moved over to the passenger seat. I pray God will take the wheel and be the driver of my life. I am blessed beyond anything I have ever imagined. I want to sing his praises all the days of my life. God has taken my tears of sorrow and changed them to shouts of joy. Glory to God in the highest!

There are many challenges ahead, and I am ready to embrace each. With God at the helm and believers surrounding me with prayers, I will venture out, trusting the journey will glorify him. For now, my job, church work, studies, and other responsibilities will continue on with a new awareness. I am grateful for my church, my pastor, and my church family of believers. I am thankful for my job and employers. My responsibilities are no longer taxing and burdensome. It is an honorable thing to work and manage life's responsibilities.

It is my mission to share my testimony through songs and prayers. I want all of God's children to share an abundant life centered in him. I want to warn them against Satan and the evils in the world.

The thief does not come except to steal, and to kill, and to destroy. I have life, and that they may have it more abundantly.

John 10:10

PART 9

Bound for the Promised Land

Greetings to all my sisters and brothers facing trials of every kind.

Life abundant is a result of obeying God's command to live in his plan. I pray my life will reflect my obedience to God, and I am dedicated to sharing the gospel through music and testaments. I pray for the success of Just Gospel. I pray it will be heard across the nation, ringing in new sounds and lifting good vibrations for lives that are flat and unmoved.

With God's help, I want to speak to young people about making better choices today by focusing on God. These kids need to hear about redeeming love. They should be warned against the evils of fast money, the lure of drugs, and self-seeking gratification. I want to promote hard work ethics based on biblical principles rather than greed. Along with the need for higher education and building good life skills, I hope to reinforce the positives of making wise choices.

Based on my own experiences, I pray that I can be candid with young men and women about the difference between love and sex. God is a better judge of character. It's important for all of us to seek God's choice for our relationships. After all, God knows a few things about "perfect love." We can trust him to choose the healthiest relationships for us.

I want to encourage moms and dads to be consistent in guiding our children to be the adults of tomorrow. The lack of parental guidance and the absence of fathers in our society are costing our children their futures. Parenting is an age-old responsibility, and we have been slacking off for too long. With God as our best example for parenting, we can love and nurture our children. We must guide them up God's highway, where they can discover his perfect design for their lives. The Bible provides the best road maps. With God's map and light shining before them, we can teach them to be contributing adults instead of takers who feel entitled.

Losing a child to death is unthinkable; it nearly killed me. I pray others never have to suffer from the loss of a child. For those who have or will lose a child, I pray my story can somehow help them recognize that our children are gifts to us from God. He has entrusted them to our care and love, whether it is for a lifetime or a life cut short. We must strive to be the best parents we can because God is counting on us. No matter if our lives follow nature's course or if that course is suddenly flipped upside down here on earth, God provides his perfect order in eternity.

Finally, I want to encourage the churches in our villages to help build spirit-filled lives. Church can offer more Bible studies where the Word can come alive to the undisciplined, the slow reader, or the lazy listener. More prayer services and small groups can help to address specific needs or problems. Worship services can be very inspiring, but what happens to us when we leave the building? How can we, the church, have a substantial impact in our villages? Churches need to offer daycare for working parents, afterschool programs that share Christ through recreation or tutoring, guidance counseling to help with developing good life skills, support groups for drug and alcohol addiction, recovery programs, divorce and marriage workshops, job fairs, and any other outreach programs that might help rebuild lives. If we can grow faithful disciples in our churches, we can heal our villages.

My life is an open book now. This is my story and this is my song, praising my Savior all the day long. I rejoice in telling my story because God told me to live, and I obeyed. Never again will the devil steal my joy. As my bishop would say, "Keep it moving and live!" As for me, I am bound for the promised land!

We are bound for the Promised Land.
We are bound for the Promised Land.
We are bound for the Promised Land,
Where we'll feast on milk and honey.
No more dark clouds, every day sunny.
We are bound, we are bound for the Promised Land.
Don't you want to come and go with me?
Don't you want to come and go with me?
Where the streets are never crowded;
Every day is howdy, howdy.
We are bound, we are bound for the Promised Land.
No more trials... Don't you want to come!
No more tribulations... Don't you want to come?
No more sickness... Don't you want to come?
No more heartache... Don't you want to come?
No more goodbyes... Don't you want to come?
For we are bound for the Promised Land!
Amen and hallelujah!

My son was murdered. During this time, I did not see the sun come up or the day change into night. I did not see the leaves change colors and fall from the trees, nor did I see the daffodils poke through the spring soil. I did not feel summer's basking heat or winter's frigid cold. These actions that prove life is in progress ceased for me except for one essential thing: my heart continued pumping blood to all the parts of my body, though I willed it to stop. As a matter of fact, that's how life went on for over fifteen years.

After the untimely death of her son, author and music artist Rikki McNeil began to ride an emotional roller coaster that constantly dipped her into the pit of despair. She began to fall into deep depression until the good Lord came along at just the right time--His timing is always perfect--and blessed her life in all the right ways.

Delve into Grace Notes and discover how Rikki overcame years of grief and rose to where she is today. Rikki is alive, not because she overcame her heartache after fifteen years, but because Christ commanded her to live.

www.ingramcontent.com/pod-product-compliance
Lightning Source LLC
LaVergne TN
LVHW011725060526
838200LV00051B/3030